WHAT OTHERS ARE SAYING

"Never before have we seen such a passionate generation of young leaders step up with a desire to change the world. The potential for change is enormous, but Greg is right when he says 'passion is not enough.' I'm excited about this book and what I believe it can do for thousands of passionate young leaders who are looking for next steps."

—PETE WILSON
Pastor of Cross Point and Author of *Plan B*.

"Many people want to change the world, but few are willing to do what it takes. I've known Greg for more than a decade and he has a message that today's young leaders need to hear. *Passion Is Not*

Enough is a healthy balance of inspiration and truth. I highly recommend this book."

—CLAYTON KING
Author of *Dying to Live*

"I work with passionate world changers all the time who hit a wall of disappointment, discouragement, and their dreams have died. Often they are faced with the hard truth that passion is simply not enough. Greg Darley lays out an insightful and honest guide about how to sustain your vision through both the valleys and mountaintops. If you truly want to scale, grow, and sustain your mission, *Passion Is Not Enough* is a must-read!"

—MIKE FOSTER
People of the Second Chance

"Passion without intentional process for implementation will quickly fade away. Too many leaders sit on their passions and ideas for far too long. Greg is an innovative leader who doesn't want to see this continue. His book, *Passion Is Not Enough*, provides a practical guide with real-life and real-time principles to inspire anyone who actually wants to live out their dreams."

—CHARLES LEE
CEO of !deation Consultancy

"You've got an idea that could change the world. Now what? *Passion Is Not Enough* will help you build the necessary foundation to move forward. This is not a ten-step program to change the world. This is sound advice that will give you encouragement on the difficult road to changing the world."

—JUD WILHITE
Author, *Throw It Down*
Senior Pastor of Central Christian Church Las Vegas

PASSION
IS NOT ENOUGH

4 Elements

to Change

the World

Greg Darley
Foreword by Mark Batterson

PASSION IS NOT ENOUGH
4 Elements to Change the World

Cover design by Stephen Bateman.

To Betsey.

To say I'm blessed with you is
an understatement. Thanks for
wanting to change the world
with me. I love you.

TABLE OF CONTENTS

ACKNOWLEDGEMENTS

Changing the world, if done alone, would be seemingly impossible, and guaranteed miserable. I am grateful for all of you.

I am first off indebted to my savior Jesus Christ for his unbelievable grace in my life. He is the giver of life and the passion behind my desire to change the world.

Betsey I am so thankful that you always believed in me, even when no one else did. Thanks for saying yes and for being the best wife ever. I love you.

Chris, thanks for being there. Through everything. Every time. I still look up to you.

Mom, thanks for demonstrating that the best way to impact the world is to serve.

Dad, thanks for encouraging my dreams, even at the cost of yours.

Mark Batterson, thanks for taking a chance on me and encouraging me to chase the lion. Your example is inspiring and I am grateful.

Mike Foster, thanks for always being in my corner. You've shown me what real influence looks like.

Chris Glynn, thanks for always helping with my ideas, especially the crazy ones.

Jennifer Schuchmann, thank you for encouraging me to write.

Robert Neely, thanks for making it look good.

Stephen Bateman, thanks for all your hard work to make this project a reality. You will accomplish great things.

Sandy Gibbes, thanks for your encouragement, creative input, and driving a cool car in college.

Charles Lee, Jeremy Cowart, Austin Guitwen, Vince Hungate, and Rob Morris, thank you for your inspiration, example, and honor of sharing your story.

My Backstage Leadership family: Lee, Angus, David, Wesley, and Frank—You guys rock! Thanks for wanting to change the world with me.

Chuck Colson and Gabe Lyons, thanks for a magnificent vision.

Clayton King, thank you for being a constant example of how to live and challenging me to go pro. I've learned so much from you.

FOREWORD

BY MARK BATTERSON

God has called us all to chase big dreams and fulfill seemingly impossible goals. He wants us to take the risk, make the jump, and go for it all. The problem for most of is not a lack of passion, talent, or faith. Our problems deal mostly with our foundation. Most of us quit too soon, especially when things get tough.

When I first discovered my *passion*, I was playing basketball for the University of Chicago on a full scholarship and felt the call to ministry. I knew God was leading me to a small bible school, but to everyone else it didn't make sense. To them, I was crazy to leave my basketball scholarship and full ride behind. But I knew that's what I needed to do. After graduation, I decided to take the risk and plant a church. God had placed in my heart the desire to make a difference. It was here that I learned that changing the world is

XII PASSION IS NOT ENOUGH

hard. The first church did not last very long. It was a challenging time for me. In the midst of shutting down my first church, God called me to our nation's capital to try again. I wasn't sure if I could go through that again, but I knew I needed to try.

On the Sunday of our very first service, the largest blizzard in recent times covered Washington with snow. I represented 50% of our attendance that day, as no one showed up. I will admit it was discouraging, but I knew what God had called me to do. It would take a lot of hard work, a lot of prayer, and a lot more work, but more than fifteen years later National Community Church has become a great influence in our capital.

For too long, Christians have let the world change them instead of them changing the world. I believe this new generation will transform that paradigm. Changing the world does not happen by having the coolest website or the largest group on Facebook. Changing the world happens when you take a risk and then commit to the process over a long period of time. What the church today desperately needs are those who are willing not only to start something but also see it through to completion.

So, what does it actually take to change the world? In the pages that follow, Greg has given us a glimpse of those who changed the world and those who are in the process. The four required elements are not easily obtained but, for those who seek, they will be found. I urge you to seek them in your quest to change the world.

I ended my book, *In a Pit with a Lion on a Snowy Day*, with the Lion Chasers Manifesto. I believe it's worth repeating here, because world changers and lion chasers are one and the same:

> Quit living as if the purpose of life is to arrive safely at death. Set God-sized goals. Pursue God-

ordained passions. Go after a dream that is destined to fail without divine intervention. Keep asking questions. Keep making mistakes. Keep seeking God. Stop pointing out problems and become part of the solution. Stop repeating the past and start creating the future. Stop playing it safe and start taking risks. Expand your horizons. Accumulate experiences. Consider the lilies. Enjoy the journey. Find every excuse you can to celebrate everything you can. Live like today is the first and last day of your life. Don't let what's wrong with you keep you from worshipping what's right with God. Burn sinful bridges. Blaze a new trail. Criticize by creating. Worry less about what people think and more about what God thinks. Don't try to be who you're not. Be yourself. Laugh at yourself. Quit holding out. Quit holding back. Quit running away. Chase the lion!

Introduction
Do Something About It

It.

What is *it*?

It is what all people who change the world have in common.

It is that thing you want to change.

It is that thing you need to change.

It is a burden.

It is a calling.

It gives you nightmares.

It is bigger than you.

It gives you passion.

It keeps you up at night.

It wakes you up in the morning.

It nags at you at work.

It comes to your mind at random times.

It is in front of you.

It is there.

It needs to be changed.

It is waiting for you.

It.

I have to do something about it!

This is what all world changers say at some point in their lives. It bothered them, so they did something about it. When Moses saw the slavery in Egypt, he had to do something about it. When Agnesë Gonxhe Bojaxhiu saw the poverty on the streets of Calcutta, India before she became known as Mother Teresa, she had to do something about it. Polio was once considered the most frightening public health problem until Jonas Salk did something about it in the mid-twentieth century and invented the first vaccination. It was nearly impossible to prosecute those who bought and sold children into slavery until Gary Haugen decided to do something about it. No one had heard the gospel in fifth-century Ireland until Patrick decided to do something about it. It propelled Chuck Colson back into prison, this time to minister. It led Pastor Diedrich Bohnhoffer to face the Nazis, and eventually death. It causes regular women and men to do extraordinary things. It causes people to change the world.

It is different for everyone. Everyone above changed the world because when they found it, they did something about it. Good intentions don't change the world. Ideas alone will change nothing. Desires don't feed the hungry. Ambition won't stop injustice.

Enthusiasm alone will not preach to the lost. Wishing changes nothing. Change requires action. Find it. Do something about it.

How do you find it?
Once you find it, what's your next move?
It seems like too big a problem. Will it really matter what you do?
Do you have what it takes to make a difference?
Will it work?
Will it be enough?

These are all questions we will explore together in this book.

It Only Took Twenty Years, But He Did It.

On the night of February 23, 1807, there were cheers all through the British House of Commons. All across the rows and in the balcony people were standing, cheering, clapping, and yelling; everyone, that is, but William Wilberforce. Twenty years before on the same floor, Wilberforce had brought his first motion to abolish the African slave trade in Great Britain and her colonies. Though his speech was passionate, even compelling, he was voted down. The same outcome of that first year happened every year for the next twenty years.

Every single year he brought forward the motion, and every year it was voted down.

Every year commitments fell through.

Every year friends backed out.

Every year something was more important.

Every year the opposition won.

Every year, that is, until this night.

After twenty years of dedication, hard work, and the fiercest of commitment, Wilberforce led the Commons to vote 283–16 in favor of abolishing the slave trade. As the vote was read aloud, the entire house erupted with cheers; Wilberforce sat and wept.

William Wilberforce not only led the fight that eventually abolished the slave trade, he led a lifelong campaign that changed the culture of an entire country—and ultimately the world. Sir Hugh Thomas wrote that the vote to abolish the slave trade was "one of the most remarkable examples of the triumph of an individual statesman on a major philanthropic issue, and at the same time one more reminder that individuals can make history."[1] Wilberforce did something about it!

Wilberforce's world is eerily similar to the world we live in today. Personal and corporate (public) morality is on a major decline. Truth is under attack. Pragmatism is king. The multi-billion dollar business scandals, the rise in divorce rates (including Christian marriages), and the billions of dollars of credit card debt are evidence of the modus operandi of *eat, drink, and be merry!* Consider the facts: half the world's population lives on less than $2 a day. Thirty thousand people die each day because they do not have access to clean water. Teenagers and young adults are leaving their faith and the church in droves.

We desperately need young Wilberforces to rise to the occasion and do something about it. In the age of tolerance, we need people to defend the truth. We need a new generation to rise up and recognize that it's not all about me! In a time when sex sells everything from hamburgers to mobile phones, we need a new generation of modesty. When video games trump learning, when the internet tops the Bible, and when friends with benefits supposedly equals a healthy relationship, will we have a new generation rise up and make history? We need this generation to do something about *it*. We need you to do something about *it*.

There is a growing movement today of people who are finding their it and doing something about it. They see it, respond to it, and the world is changing as a result. In our time together, we'll look behind the scenes at some people who changed the world, or who are in the middle of changing it. We'll look at the key elements required to change the world. We'll look at many true stories of those changing the world, including those as young as nine years old! Changing the world is not easy. If you asked any of these people if it was easy, they would all say *no*! If you asked them if it was worth it, every one of them would say absolutely *yes*! It will be worth it.

How Do We Change the World?

This book is about YOU finding it and then changing the world. Some of you already have a burden, but now it's time to do something about it. Some of you are already doing something about it. That's great. This book will help you achieve long-term success. Some of you need a burden, like the issue of slavery. Still others will get burdens for local needs, single moms, orphans, cancer victims, planting a church, talking to your parents about Jesus, or any number of a thousand ways to change the world. My belief, though, is that everyone is called to change the world. That means YOU. Once you find your it, you will have to do something about it.

So, what will it take to do something about it?

What does it take to change the world?

There are four elements you will need to change the world, each one building on the next. Please note, this is not a "how to change the world in four easy steps" book. If anything, this is a "how to change the world with four tough and long steps" book. However, don't let that scare you away. Each one is actually more than a single step. Each element will need to be continually renewed.

If you like to stay physically fit, you know that working out is not a one-time event. It is a continual process. In much the same way, to see the greatest results, the elements to changing the world will take continual effort. We will discuss what each one is, why it's important, and how to get it.

Ultimately this book is about leadership. Now, I wouldn't say this is a leadership book per se, but in its essence changing the world requires that you lead some type of change. If the change is in your neighborhood or across an entire continent, it will require you to lead. But you need to know that having a passion to change something is not enough. Passion is necessary, but you need four additional elements to make the change you desire possible.

The four elements are:

1. **Calling:** This is the motivation and goal behind what you want to change. Calling is about finding your it. This is your burden.
2. **Character:** If people don't respect, trust, and believe in you, they won't help you change the world. Your character is vital to long-term success, because how you change the world is as important as actually changing it.

3. **Doctrine:** These are the beliefs that will anchor you during tough times, and believe me, it will be tough. Doctrine is what anchors your it to the way God is working to change the world.

4. **Commitment:** This element includes preparation, effort, and dedication over an extended period of time.

Do you have an idea or dream you'd love to accomplish?

Do you think about making an impact on your community, or even changing the world?

Do you want to know how to accomplish your biggest dreams? Keep reading and join me in doing something about it!

CALLING

CHAPTER 1
WHAT HANGS IN THE BALANCE

*"Unless someone like you cares a
whole awful lot, nothing is going
to get better. It's not."*
—DR. SEUSS

A Billion and Counting

This past year, my wife and I were visiting her family in Charlotte, North Carolina over a weekend. Besides being the home of my adorable nieces and nephews, Charlotte houses the Billy Graham Memorial Library and Museum. Having never visited before, we agreed to go along for an afternoon tour and picnic. Set on a beautiful piece of quiet property with full-grown trees and gorgeous landscaping, the museum is a walking biography through the life of Billy from his childhood to today. You start out by listening to a talking cow introduce the tour. Next, you pass through a replica of an old house, and then into a 1950s television studio. Billy was known for pushing the envelope of technology to spread his message. There's one section of the tour dedicated to some of Billy's most memorable crusades.

For more than fifty years, Billy traveled the world preaching the gospel to millions of people in tents, stadiums, and open fields. I was struck by the picture of a crusade that took place in South Korea in the 1970s. The image from the stage showed a crowd of close to one million people with the last row nowhere in sight. In a three-day stretch, he preached to three million people live—and in person! Later we learned that over the course of his life he reached over a billion people, live. That's billion with a "B." And that does not include the number of people who watched him preach on TV. After walking through the museum, it was blatantly evident that Billy Graham changed the world.

As we were leaving that day, I was struck by the question— *What if he had refused to be an evangelist?* What if he had continued with the family business or tried his hand at something else, like acting? The decision he faced was no different from the one many of you will have to make. You have options, like a family business or being a lawyer because everyone in your family is a lawyer. Consider how different the world would have been if Billy had ignored his call to do something about it. You most likely know someone who heard the gospel for the first time because of Billy Graham. If Billy ignored the call, who would have filled his shoes? After seeing the number of people who were impacted by his ministry, I realized that if he had not have embraced God's call, more than a billion people might have missed out on hearing the gospel.

More than a billion! What if Billy had said no? If not Billy, who would have done it? What if more than a billion people's future hung in the balance, their futures hinging on your decision to do something about it?

It's Alright, It's Alright

There's a famous saying that many assume is in the Bible (it's actually not) that says, "God moves in mysterious ways." It's one of those clichés that pastors or news anchors use when they can't explain why something happened. "It seems that this giant truck broke down with exactly enough chili for the annual local chili festival. Since the grocery stores are on strike, we wouldn't have had any chili otherwise. Yep, God moves in mysterious ways!"

Every time I hear that line, I think of the U2 song *Mysterious Ways.* (I'm now singing it as I type. Feel free to sing along.) God may very well move in mysterious ways, but he also moves in strategic ways. When it comes to planning, there is no one better than God. He successfully manages six billion people, seven continents, four hemispheres, and a hundred gazillion prayers everyday. He knows which person needs to move where, and when, and who will be born today, and what each one of them will grow up to do, how that will have a profound impact on those people, which will affect this guy, and that girl, who will then decide to try this stuff, which will help even more people over there, and so on and so on. Got that?

In God's providential order of the universe, he has perfectly positioned you to accomplish the calling he has given you—or the one he will give you. And that call is to change the world. Think about that for a moment. You are perfectly positioned. God is perfect with details and logistics. He knows the gifts and talents you'll need to do something about it. He knows the people you'll need around you and the people you'll need to learn from. He knows what education you'll need and what city you should live in. For all those dots you worry about, God has connected them perfectly. A lot hangs in the balance of your calling, so God is working on connecting the dots.

So, if he calls you to plant a church, he has worked out the details of how you will do it, who will come the first week, and who will come the five hundred and first week. If he calls you to start a neighborhood Bible study, he knows who will come and how they'll be impacted. If he calls you to be a teacher, start a business, become a missionary, direct movies in Hollywood, or any number of other possibilities, remember two things. One, he will perfectly position you to accomplish your calling. Two, that calling is to change the world—it's not just about you. In the case of Billy Graham, his decision to accept God's call to change the world affected a billion people, not just himself and his family. The same goes for you. Your decision to embrace or ignore your call to change the world will always affect more people than just you.

Butterfly Effect

You may not be the next Billy Graham. You may not want to be. Either way, God has given all of us the same call to change the world. This means we have to take all our focus off ourselves and look out in the world and see where we can make a difference. Your decision will never affect just you. It will always affect countless other people, who will in turn affect other people, who will in turn affect other people.

This reminds me of the Butterfly Effect theory, coined by Edward Lorenz. According to Wikipedia, "The butterfly effect is a metaphor that encapsulates the concept of sensitive dependence on initial conditions in chaos theory; namely that small differences in the initial condition of a dynamical system may produce large variations in the long term behavior of the system." Basically, the theory says that if a butterfly flaps its wings in Brazil, it could cause a tornado in Texas.[2]

Can a little butterfly actually cause a tornado? Wikipedia says, "The flapping wing represents a small change in the initial condition of the system, which causes a chain of events leading to large-scale alterations of events. Had the butterfly not flapped its wings, the trajectory of the system might have been vastly different. While the butterfly does not 'cause' the tornado in the sense of providing the energy for the tornado, it does 'cause' it in the sense that the flap of its wings is an essential part of the initial conditions resulting in a tornado, and without that flap that particular tornado would not have existed."[3] The idea is that the little inputs lead to potentially huge outcomes. Billy Graham accepting the call to preach was a butterfly flap that led to a billion people hearing the gospel. All decisions have a butterfly effect.

The Game That Changed My Life

There's a group of men and women who are responsible for my marriage, and I don't know them. In the year 2000, a group of delegates met to vote on who they would invite from the ACC to play in the Gator Bowl in Jacksonville, Florida. Because of the standings in the conference, including the win-loss breakdown among teams and what teams were taken by other bowl committees, the

Gator Bowl delegates selected Clemson University to come to Florida. At the time, I was a sophomore at Clemson, and a group of friends decided we'd drive the seven hours to celebrate New Year's in Jacksonville and take in the football game. We crammed fifteen people into two Motel 6 rooms and had a memorable few days. But little did I know that my future would forever be changed.

After Clemson got destroyed in the game, my older brother Chris, who was also down for the game, called and wanted to know if I wanted to stay a few more days in Florida and hang out with some of his friends. Having nothing better to do, I parted with my roommates and headed across town to meet up with him. When I caught up with my brother, with him were a bunch of his friends from Clemson, but there was only one who I was interested in. Chris introduced me to his friend's sister, whose house we would be staying at. She was beautiful, and four years later, when we said "I do," I became a regular in that same house. People ask me all the time why I'm so passionate about Clemson football. Now you know.

What would have happened if Clemson had lost one more game that year? Would they have been invited to the Gator Bowl? If not, would I have ever met Betsey? Would we still have gotten married? I am grateful for the team that year, for the Gator Bowl selection committee, and for my brother asking me to hang out a few extra days. If not, I might have missed the love of my life. A lot hung in the balance of that one football game. The delegates' decision affected a lot more people than they'll ever know. The same is true of your decision. A lot hangs in the balance.

Remember, Remember

A powerful movie came out a few years ago with Natalie Portman called *V for Vendetta*. It presents a "what-if" scenario showing what might have happened if the Nazis had won World War II. In the movie, Britain is a socialist regime where there is no freedom. All information is censored and no one knows the truth of their humanity. It is a powerful reminder of how terrible the world could be if certain men and women had not embraced their call to change the world.

I can't help but to think about the opening scene of *Saving Private Ryan*, the one with the Marines storming the beaches of Normandy. Men were getting mowed down by machine guns as soon as they hit the beach. An estimated ten thousand people were injured or killed that day in what would become the turning point in the war and lead to the end of the Nazi regime. But what would have happened if those men had ignored the call to storm the beach? What would have happened if they had thought, "Not me. I'm sure someone else will do it." History does not afford us the answer, but *V for Vendetta* paints a possibility that is riveting and scary.

Think about the number of lives that hung in the balance, that depended on the Allies winning the war. We know that at least six million Jews died at Nazi hands. Think about how many more could have died. Looking back, we see that there was more at stake than the lives of the men who stormed the beaches of Normandy—there was an entire continent at stake, an entire race. A lot hung in the balance of that one battle.

The Story You Always Wanted

A few years ago, my wife and I had the opportunity to travel to northern Europe to visit some cities in Scandinavia. One of the things we both love to do on trips is to take pictures—lots and lots of pictures. For a weeklong trip, we can take as many as a few thousand pictures to showcase our memories. On this particular trip, we first flew into London for a few days, then took a cruise ship into the Baltic Sea, where our first stop was Stockholm, Sweden.

If you have ever been to London, you know how much there is to see and do. We took a double-decker tour bus and saw Big Ben, Parliament, London Bridge, St. Paul's, and everything in between. After a day and a half, we easily had four hundred pictures. We were having the time of our lives and had plenty of pictures to prove it.

The next day, we arrived in Stockholm and took a river cruise through the city. Stockholm was beautiful. So beautiful, in fact, that we took hundreds of pictures. Our favorite stop was the Ice Bar, located downtown in the lobby of the Nordic Sea hotel. Upon entering the Ice Bar, we were given thermal jackets and gloves to put on because it is 23 degrees Fahrenheit inside! Everything was made of ice. The floor, the walls, the bar, the stools, and even the glasses—all ice. Pardon the pun, but it was very cool!

After leaving the Ice Bar, we did some more sightseeing downtown, then jumped on our tour bus, which dropped us back at the port in time to get on the cruise ship. When we got back to our room on the boat, the day took a turn for the worst. Betsey was looking in the closet, and I lay down on the bed.

"Hey, let me see the camera. I want to look at the pictures from today," I said.

She stuck her head out from behind the closet door and said, "I don't have it. I thought you had it."

"No, I don't have it. You had it when we got on the bus," I corrected her.

She felt all her pockets and shook her head. "I don't have it. Check the bag."

I grabbed the backpack and pulled out our water bottles, tour guides, and sunscreen. And at the bottom of the bag was nothing. Our camera was gone.

"Oh *no!* I must have left it on the bus. It's not here!" I said. "Come on. I'm going to run back to the bus and look there."

I grabbed my key card and we bolted for the door. We raced down to the bus drop-off point to see that there were at least thirty buses coming and going. We found someone with a walkie-talkie and asked if there was a way to call the driver of our bus.

The person asked, "What number was your bus?"

"I think it was 14. We came from the city center. It was only a few minutes ago," Betsey said.

I was looking around at all the buses, and then reality hit. Over the radio we heard, "That bus is already gone, and the driver cannot come back to the port."

"I'm sorry. That bus has already been turned in," the gentleman with the walkie-talkie said. "We will ask them to look on the bus for you. If we find it, we can mail it to you."

We gave the guy our email address and walked slowly back to the ship. "I don't know where I left it," I said. "I remember having it there at the capital building right before we jumped on the bus. It has to be on that bus."

And there it was… the truth hitting me in the gut. Our camera, with all our pictures of the first four days of our trip, was gone. I was crushed. Not only did I lose all the pictures, but now there would be no camera to take pictures of the rest of our trip. The next morning we stopped in Helsinki, Finland. Betsey and I decided not to go on a tour through the cruise ship; instead, we chose to walk around town. When we got downtown, Betsey said, "Look at that," and pointed to a billboard advertising Canon cameras.

"Like I need to be reminded about yesterday. That's like pouring salt in the wound," I said.

Just twenty-four hours earlier, we owned a Canon camera, but now a Swedish bus driver was enjoying it. Betsey knew how much taking pictures meant to me. She could tell I was still upset and, on a whim, said, "Come on, let's go get a camera."

She grabbed my hand and we ran into the Finish equivalent of a Service Merchandise. (Are those even around anymore?) We ended up buying an overpriced camera, but at that point it didn't matter because we were forever going to remember our trip.

When we got our shiny new camera out of the box, we realized we were in a little bit of trouble. "Hey, look at this," I said.

Handing the camera to Betsey, she tried to read the opening menu with as little success as I had.

"It's in Finnish, isn't it?" she said.

I looked at Betsey and we started to laugh. "I guess so."

We walked up to numerous people, trying to find someone who spoke English and could read Finnish to change the menu to English so we could work the camera. We finally found someone to help us. We went on to explore the city and had a great time laughing about our new camera. Every time I see that camera today, I think about that moment. It doesn't hurt that the outside of the camera has nothing but Finnish writing on it either, which adds to the story when people try to read it. "Oh, you don't read Finn?"

At the time, that was not a funny story. Looking back, however, we will never forget our time in Finland. It is forever etched into our minds. And that is exactly the type of life you were called to live. One with great memories. And the greatest memories come from great stories. Donald Miller does a wonderful job with this concept in his book *A Million Miles in a Thousand Years*. He says that a life of meaningful stories will be remembered as a meaningful life.

We said earlier that millions, or even billions, of people's lives and eternity hang in the balance of your decision to accept the call to change the world. But something else hangs in the balance of your decisions as well—your own life. Do you want a life that looks like everyone else's around you? Do you want a life where your only stories are about going to work, coming home, watching TV, and doing it all again the next day? Or do you want a life that has great meaning and purpose, one where you are energized by what you do and how you spend your time? A life filled with stories forever etched into your memories, and also the memories of others, is a life focused on doing something about *it*.

But…

When your it comes calling, the normal human response is to immediately list all the reasons why you cannot do something about it.

I'm not old enough.

I'm too old.

I have a family.

I don't have a family.

I'm too poor.

I'm too rich.

I'm not qualified.

I've never been overseas.

I don't know the language.

I stutter.

I'm not smart enough.

I don't have a degree.

I'm a drop-out.

I'm a teenager.

I'm divorced.

I'm a woman.

I'm a minority.

I'm a man.

I've never started anything before.

I'm crippled.

The list could literally go on forever. Every idea to change the world comes equipped with unlimited excuses. How you handle those excuses will correlate directly with your ability to change the world.

What excuses are you using?

"You'll most likely never walk again." This is what one man heard in his attempt to do something about it. Polio was killing his body, so friends and family told Frank that he should forget about politics. "No one will vote for a cripple," they told him. As far as excuses go, this was as good as any. Walking is pretty important to be the leader of a nation, but don't tell that to the thirty-second president of the United States. For most of his presidency, Franklin Roosevelt wore forty-pound braces on both his legs, but that didn't stop him from leading the nation through the dark times of the Depression and World War II. Roosevelt would not let his legs slow him down in his process to do something about it. The future of entire continents hung in the balance of his decisions. When the excuses come calling, tell them to take a hike. The world is not changed by excuse makers but by those who figure out a way around them.

Our Call Is Still the Same

Back in the Garden of Eden, God gave Adam the call to do something meaningful with his life. God told Adam to create and cultivate the creation—in our terms, to change the world. Even when sin brought death and destruction to the Earth, the call to change the world remained.

We are still called to do something meaningful with our lives, not just to get by. When we pursue the call to change the world, we begin to live the life that Jesus had in mind in John 10:10. He told the disciples that the thief comes to steal, kill, and destroy, but he came so that they might have life to the full, or life abundantly. I like how the Message translates the passage: *"I came so they can have real and eternal life, more and better life than they ever dreamed of"* (The Message). A life better than you ever dreamed of is one where you spend your time making memories that matter, where people are served, marriages restored, hungry people fed, slaves set free, and lives changed forever.

So we see that we are called to change the world, and when we do, we are actually living the life God has called us to live. A lot hangs in the balance of your willingness to accept this call. In our time together, you'll read stories about men and woman just like you who chose to do something about it. They probably didn't realize it at the time, but millions of lives hung in the balance of their decision to do something about *it*. The same is true for you. If you will embrace the call to do something about *it*, you could change millions of lives.

CHAPTER 2
UNCOVERING CALLING

*"If you can't feed a hundred
people, then feed just one."*
—MOTHER TERESA

A Shot of Hope

A few years ago, I was attending the Catalyst Conference in Atlanta, Georgia—a gathering of twelve thousand leaders from across the country who come together for three days of learning, worship, and inspiration. The days are filled with legendary speakers who have accomplished amazing things, written best-selling books, preached to thousands of people, and built successful businesses, churches, and non-profits. In short, their resumes are pretty impressive. And in between all that, a twelve-year-old kid walked out on stage for an interview.

Austin Gutwein decided he wanted to change the world. At age nine, Austin watched a video showing children who had lost their parents to the AIDS virus. After finishing the short movie, he told his parents he knew he needed to do something about it. These kids were his age. By the time he got home from school that day, another two thousand kids would be orphaned. Austin had found his passion and his idea. And he was nine! So what do you do when you find it and you are nine? The same thing you do if you are nineteen or twenty-nine or fifty-nine: you do something about it with what you have, where you are.

For Austin, this meant basketball. Basketball was his love. On World AIDS Day, Austin got friends and family to sponsor him to shoot free throws, one for every kid who would be orphaned that day due to AIDS. At the end of the day, Austin shot 2,057 free throws and raised almost $3000. The next year, Austin recruited friends and other schools to join him, and out of their success, the Hoops of Hope shoot-a-thon was born. Together they raised $35,000. The following year, $85,000. The next year, $211,000. The year after that, $405,000. Since the first free throw Austin took at age nine, he has mobilized tens of thousands of kids to raise more than $2 million to benefit those affected by AIDS. Now those sick with the disease have a clinic to get treatments, a school to attend, and a better chance of survival. If it hadn't been for Austin, how many more orphans would have died? Austin did something about it.

Where to Look

Many of you can identify with Austin immediately. You've had that moment where you watched a video or read a story about an issue, and it broke your heart. You just knew you needed to do something about it. But others haven't had that moment. Or, if you have, it wasn't as clear as you'd hoped. So, what do you do then? You want to change the world, but you just don't know how. One of the best decisions you can make then is to dig in until you find it, and the best place to start is in the Scriptures. In Matthew, we see a great example of how Jesus did ministry. Jesus was in the prime of his ministry. It says, *"Jesus went through all the towns and villages, teaching in their synagogues, preaching the good news of the kingdom and healing every disease and sickness"* (Matthew 9:35). Let's break down this verse to further our pursuit of uncovering our calling.

The first idea we see is that Jesus was on the move. He was in one town one day and another the next. He was being exposed to new environments and new people. One of the best things you can do is to get out of town, or at least on the other side of town. If you spend your time in the same places with the same people, your burdens will rarely change. Take a visit to your local hospital, volunteer at an inner city elementary school, or try a food bank. If you can afford it, you need to go overseas and see what extreme poverty looks like. I would say that you truly cannot afford not to go. Once you stand in an African slum and stare into the face of poverty, you will be both thankful and motivated for change. You must expose yourself to different environments, new people, and real information. Spend an afternoon Googling poverty, slavery, or

AIDS. Read stories about orphans or victims of a hurricane. Find out how many single parents live in your school district. Ask your local school how many students need help with basic skills like reading and writing. If nothing grips your heart, keep searching.

In 1865, William Booth, former Methodist minister, established the East London Christian Mission. Its purpose was to help the poor and destitute with their physical and spiritual needs. Booth's mission was to provide the three 'S's—soup, soap, and salvation. Booth knew that a person would not listen to a sermon if he was listening to his stomach. Booth also knew that a person would more likely respond to a message of grace if he was clean. After the first two conditions were met, Booth knew the time was ripe to preach the gospel. By 2009, Booth's ministry was located in 118 countries around the world, impacting millions of people every year and raising more than $3 billion.

Today you know his ministry as the Salvation Army. Booth recognized the impact that meeting physical needs has on one's ability to preach the gospel. This example is from Jesus, who went from town to town preaching *and* healing diseases and sickness and, on numerous occasions, feeding the hungry.

Good Use for a Quarter

I was talking with Charles, a good friend, the other day about how his church was ministering to the homeless in his area. Charles lives outside of Los Angeles and the homeless population is surprisingly high.

"Just dropping off a sack lunch has limiting effect and shows that we don't really understand the issue," he said.

"So what is a better way to do something about it?" I asked him.

"Well, with the help of some friends at another church, we launched a simple project to show love to the homeless and offer practical help; we called it Laundry Love. On Saturdays, we get a group from our churches and take over coin laundromats in our area."

"What do you mean, you take them over?" I asked.

"Basically, we go in and wash clothes for the homeless. Many times we provide lunch and games for children. By spending a few hours together washing clothes and eating lunch every few weeks, we've built real relationships and seen real life change. Having clean clothes is something you don't think about too often when dealing with homelessness. Food is always the default, but having on a clean shirt means a lot. It makes people feel human again. For many homeless students, we've found they hate going to school wearing the same dirty clothes all the time. By washing a load of clothes, we've seen more students get back into the classroom."

"I've never even thought about that," I said. "Clean clothes are just something you take for granted. So, how many people have been affected with Laundry Love?"

"After seeing how successful the local Laundry Love events were, we put the project online to empower others to do the same. We put up ideas on how to raise money, spread the word, and raise volunteers. One of the first groups to embrace it placed gumball machines in their area and used the quarters on Laundry Love day. So, after about two years, there are at least 75 different Laundry Love locations around the country with 20,000 people being served each month! And those are just the ones we know about," he said. "Some people don't report their numbers or they take the idea and call it something else. We're completely fine with that, as long as people are being served."

Laundry Love was a simple idea to show love to people. Charles and his team are changing the world one load of clothes at a time.

After Matthew tells us that Jesus was going from town to town preaching and healing people, he shows us the condition of Jesus' heart. If this is the way you feel, your problem won't be finding *one* it; it will be deciding which one to pursue. Matthew writes, *"When he [Jesus] saw the crowds, he had compassion on them, because they were harassed and helpless, like sheep without a shepherd"* (Matthew 9:36).

Crowds can be scary. I know some people who cannot stand to be in a crowd. They freak out with all the bumping and knocking shoulders. Scientists call this fear of large crowds enochlophobia. It can be paralyzing to be surrounded by that many people. Jesus was not afraid of the crowds. In fact, he embraced them. When Jesus saw the crowds, his heart felt compassion. True compassion is when you not only recognize someone else's pain but you actually hurt with them. Their pain becomes your pain. This is what happened when Jesus saw the crowds. Their pain, problems, and misfortunes became his. When you are in pain, you cannot ignore it. You must seek a remedy. When you have compassion for someone, you must seek a remedy for that pain as if it were yours. That is the example Jesus gave us.

When Everything Changed

"If you don't think you can stomach this, you need to stay here." That was Rob's warning as they were standing outside a house one cool evening.

"There will be little girls in here for sale *and* there will be guys buying them. But you cannot act on your impulses. You cannot say something. We're still investigating this place, so you cannot do anything to blow our cover. If you see something you are not able to deal with, you must keep your emotions together."

This was what Rob was told just before he went undercover with investigators in a brothel that sold children as prostitutes. As part of an ongoing investigation, Rob, co-founder of Love 146, saw firsthand the injustice of child sex slavery.

This is the story that changed his life. In his own words:

> We found ourselves standing shoulder to shoulder with predators in a small room, looking at little girls through a pane of glass. All of the girls wore red dresses with a number pinned to their dress for identification. They sat, blankly watching cartoons on TV. They were vacant shells of what a child should be. There was no light in their eyes, no life left. Their light had been taken from them. These children... raped each night... seven, ten, fifteen times every night. They were so young. Thirteen, eleven... it was hard to tell. Sorrow covered their faces with nothingness. Except one girl. One girl who wouldn't watch the cartoons. Her number was 146. She was looking beyond the glass. She was

staring out at us with a piercing gaze. There was still fight left in her eyes. There was still life left in this girl...

All of these emotions begin to wreck you. Break you. It is agony. It is aching. It is grief. It is sorrow. The reaction is intuitive, instinctive. It is visceral. It releases a wailing cry inside of you. It elicits gut-level indignation. It is unbearable. I remember wanting to break through the glass. To take her away from that place. To scoop up as many of them as I could into my arms. To take all of them away. I wanted to break through the glass to tell her to keep fighting. To not give up. To tell her that we were coming for her...

Because we went in as part of an ongoing, undercover investigation on this particular brothel, we were unable to immediately respond. Evidence had to be collected in order to bring about a raid, and eventually justice, on those running the brothel. It is an immensely difficult problem when an immediate response cannot address an emergency. Sometime later, there was a raid on this brothel and children were rescued. But the girl who wore #146 was no longer there. We do not know what happened to her, but we will never forget her. She changed the course of all our lives.

Do I Have to Start a Ministry?

At this point, you may be thinking that very question. Are you telling me I have to start a ministry? The answer is absolutely *no*. I'm not saying you need to quit your job, change careers, and start a ministry. The point is for you to discover your God-given calling and passion and pursue it. This could be teaching, architecture, practicing law, writing, helping single moms, volunteering, or teaching guitar lessons. But we must recognize that all these passions can and should be used to change the world. Charles' Laundry Love project was a simple way for him to serve his city on the weekends; it was not a full-time job. There are plenty of ways to make an impact while staying in your current job. So, if you still don't know what your next step should be, answer these questions:

- Where are my talents and strengths?
- What do I do that makes me feel alive inside?
- Is there a way to combine the two and leverage them to change the world?

What Are My Talents and Strengths?

Are you good at math? What about web design? Are you good at starting new things? Do you manage people well? Can you give a killer presentation or write well-defined essays? Are you good with cars or typing? Are sports your thing? What are the areas you are talented in?

Take a few minutes and write down a few answers. Everyone is talented at something. All of your strengths are given to you for a reason. When answering this question, don't sell yourself short or think you are being conceited. If you are good at business, write it down. If you are a compassionate person, write it down. If you are the best teacher in the school, write it down. Are you a talented musician, writer, or designer? If you are having trouble or just want another opinion, ask a few people you trust. Ask a friend, co-worker, roommate, spouse, sibling, or your boss. Be sure to ask people who will speak truthfully to you. You need honest, raw feedback. Once you've figured that out, move to the next question.

What Makes Me Come Alive?

I hate keeping records. I'm not sure if there's anything worse than balancing books to file taxes. Keeping receipts and spreadsheets and file folders is like pulling teeth, getting a shot, and then being punched in the face. Well, for me, anyway. Maybe those things make you come alive. At the mere mention of spreadsheets and file folders, your heart skips a beat. You were excited and looked over at your organized file cabinets and sighed. If that's you, you should know that people like me don't understand you at all, but we love you. If I didn't have someone help me, I'd never be able to pay any bills on time, nor would I have a clue on how my financials stood. Bless all of you organization freaks!

Now, if that makes you come alive—I mean, you really get jacked up about spending your time doing it—then you're on to something. If you would do it free, you're knocking on the right door. If you get finished for a day or complete a project and you don't know where the time has gone, you're getting even closer. Doing something that makes you come alive is fueling, not draining. It gives you joy and energy. Now, it will still be hard work, but it will be rewarding work. You will gladly sweat for something that matters to you.

So, what makes you come alive? Is it designing websites, teaching kids to read, public speaking, writing, starting companies, selling insurance, or coaching high school football? Is it helping stop injustice like slavery, building clean water wells, volunteering

at an AIDS clinic, or building orphanages? Look back over the past
year. Are there times that stick out the most? What were you doing? The goal is to identify activities that you get joy from doing.

Leverage

There are two ways to combine your strengths and what makes
you come alive to change the world. The first way is to use leverage. This is about doing what you are good at, which allows you to
then change the world. Think about how Bill Gates has leveraged
his success with Microsoft to do something about malaria, which
kills thousands of people around the world each day. Jimmy Carter
has leveraged his personal influence as former president to promote the work of Habitat for Humanity. Leveraging is about using
your strengths and talents in a way that benefits others. This could
be your job, a skill, your personality, your business, your brand, or
your connections.

Bill is a friend of mine who is a brilliant strategy consultant
working with major corporations in the S&P 500. He helps think
through major decisions for the company. He loves his job and it
provides a good living for his family, and he's good at what he
does. But that's not what makes him come alive. What makes him
come alive is using his gifts to help companies create social good.

For example, he worked with a food company that developed
a protein-rich product that could be cheaply produced to help
those suffering in third-world countries. He leveraged his strength,
and as a result tens of thousands of malnourished children get to
eat. He is not able to do that full-time, but it makes working even
more enjoyable because working creates opportunities to leverage
his skills for the greater good. If he had not pursued what he was

good at and what he was passionate about, potentially thousands of people would have died from malnutrition.

Jason is another friend who owns and operates a Chick-fil-A franchise outside Atlanta, Georgia. His day job is to run a restaurant. He has more than sixty staff to supervise, plus inventory to manage, not to mention all the legal issues of running a business. He happens to be really good at his job and sells a lot of chicken. This is his strength and he loves it, but that's not his biggest passion. His biggest passion is to leverage that strength to help build schools in Niger. Through selling chicken sandwiches, Jason is able to bring huge life change to villages halfway around the world.

Is there something you can do to leverage opportunities to make a difference? You have been entrusted to use what you're good at for something greater than yourself.

Merge

The second way to combine your strengths and what makes you come alive is to merge the two completely. Take what you are good at and what makes you come alive—and do them together.

Korey, one of my oldest friends, had a huge passion for football. From early elementary school through high school he was considered one of the hardest working players on his team. He lived and breathed football. His unrivaled levels of passion for the game, which showed up on game day, eventually led to the state championship during our junior year of high school. When it was apparent that his playing career would not extend to college, he decided to pursue a degree in education. Why education? Because with an education degree he returned to teach high school history and also be the assistant head coach. He gets to pour his gifts into the lives of hundreds of students each year, sharing his passion for the game of football. But that passion extends further; he also gets to teach valuable lessons that will extend well after his players' careers are over.

Dustin is a great friend from college who has a strength in public speaking and leadership. He also has a passion to share the gospel with those who have never heard it. The most natural thing he could do is merge those two, which he did when he planted a church more than five years ago. Now, he uses his strengths every week to preach sermons and lead his church staff. When combined with his passion to share the gospel, he sees great results. Do you have strengths and passions that you can merge?

List your areas of strengths and areas of passion and see if there are any natural fits. Get a few trusted friends to look at your list and brainstorm some ideas. Find connections between the lists. Merging the two will be a powerful way to live and change the world.

What Would You Do If You Were Certain You Wouldn't Fail?

How would you answer that question? Is there something you dream about and wish you could pursue? Is there an idea or issue that pops into your mind that you push away, thinking you could never do anything about it? But what if you were certain that you couldn't fail; would you then try? I think you would, and I think you should. Sometimes your *it* is right in front of you. When you get an inkling to do something that would serve people, help people, love people, and show compassion to people—you can be certain God is with you. You might not get the results you are expecting, but God is with you. Whenever you serve someone, you are changing his or her world.

A final word of caution: once you get a passion for what could be and should be, you need to pursue it with everything you have. Once a passion ignites inside of you, you need to fan that flame and let it consume you. The worst mistake you can make is to birth a passion and then let it dwindle. Doing this will leave you with regret. You will always wonder what it would have been like to pursue that dream. You will look back and wish you had gone for it. Remember, a lot hangs in the balance of your decision to pursue your God-given passion. You need to go for it. The *world* needs you to go for it.

For those who are still uncertain about what to pursue, you need to keep looking. Get out of your comfort zone. Find the most passionate person you know and spend time with them. Passionate people are contagious. They can't help but give you a piece of their passion. By spending time with them, their passion may easily become your passion, or at the very least they may awaken something new inside you. Passion always gives birth to passion. Go find yours!

CHARACTER

CHAPTER 3
GUARDING YOUR CHARACTER

"You must be the change you
wish to see in the world."
—MAHATMA GHANDI

The Scandal of All Scandals

It had been a tough year for America as the military had just come home from a long and deadly war. People were hurting. Homes were destroyed. Families were lost. The country needed something to hold it together. People needed something to believe in again. The year was 1919, and America needed baseball.

For those in Chicago, it had been a nearly perfect season. Charles Comiskey, the owner of the White Sox, had assembled

one of the greatest lineups in history. On paper, his squad destroyed the competition nearly every time. Going into the World
Series, the White Sox were heavy favorites to beat the Cincinnati
Reds. If the odds were right, the Reds didn't have a chance. The
White Sox were just that good. But that was on paper. The day
before Game One of the Series, the odds started shifting greatly in
favor of the Reds. The only explanation for this was that more
money was being bet on a Reds victory than on the White Sox.

Unbeknownst to Comiskey, or even most of the White Sox
players themselves, there was a plot to ruin it all. First baseman
Chuck Gandil was secretly meeting with petty gamblers leading up
to Game One. He put together a plan to make $20,000, more than
tripling his salary. With the help of seven other players, he would
intentionally lose the World Series.

On the morning of Game One, the odds were closing in despite the obvious differences in talent on the field. This shift in the
odds made no sense to anyone, except for a few gamblers and
eight Chicago White Sox players. After being heavy favorites, Kid
Gleason, the White Sox manager, had no idea how his ball club
had managed to lose the first two games. It just didn't make sense.
He had heard the rumors, but certainly they weren't true.

After the final game, few realized the extent that eight ball
players would forever leave on Major League baseball. The players
had successfully thrown the biggest sporting event in the world—
all to make a few extra bucks. But despite the rumors, nothing
came to light. No one really believed the Series had been fixed. Or
at least, no one wanted to. But then evidence began to mount, and
a Grand Jury was commissioned to set matters straight. During the
following season, all eight Chicago White Sox players would be
tried. Even though many confessed, a strange number of events

allowed the players to be acquitted. But there was no way to hide the fact that the Series had been thrown. Even though formally found innocent, all eight players were suspended for the season and later banned from Major League baseball for life. Some players, including Shoeless Joe Jackson, denied having any involvement in the scandal, but nonetheless they were still held accountable.

The story of the 1919 "Black Sox," as they would later become known, put a blemish on the game of baseball for decades. The actions of a few men affected the entire nation. But how did it ever get that far? How could a group of men justify their actions and deceive millions of people? In this case, as in many other cases like it, the talent and greed of the players proved more than their character could sustain.

Between you and me, I don't think you'll ever have the chance to throw the World Series. And if you do, I hope you are smart enough to realize that you will be caught. If the players got caught in 1919 with no TV or Internet, how fast would you get caught now? This is not a tip on deciding which sporting event to throw. The point of this story is that every single one of us will face the temptation to compromise our character along our path to change the world. There will be an opportunity for you to cut corners, make a shady deal, or dance around in some gray areas. You'll have an opportunity to cross a line and nobody will know. Or will they? You'll face a crossroads with two choices. The first will take you where you think you want to go more quickly and easily. The second will eventually get you where you want to go, but it will probably be a harder and longer journey. If you want to change the world, you need to build a solid foundation. Your character takes a long time to build and a short time to lose.

Change Begins with You

All change starts with one person. Every single point of change in the history of the world can be traced back to a beginning with a single individual. Were there times when people worked together to change something, like the Wright brothers changing the face of travel? Sure. I didn't say change only happens through one individual—I said it starts there. It starts as a dream in someone's heart. It begins as a discontentment in the mind of an individual. It always begins with a person and then spreads to those around him. This is why, if you sense a burden to change the world in any fashion, you must first pursue that change in yourself. It doesn't matter if you want to change the world, or even your marriage, family, community, or school—the change first must come to you. You simply cannot change anything before you change you. T.M. Moore said, "Transformed people transform cultures." It all begins with you.

This is a very important concept to understand, because people will not support your vision of changing the world unless they trust you. Moral failure is the number one reason people lose faith in a leader. Think about that for a moment.

Would you work for someone who stole from you?

Would you work for someone who lied to you?

Would you give hours of your week for a leader like that?

How long would you work for someone who scolded you for being late but was consistently late himself?

Would you give money to a charity if you knew the leader was putting half in his pocket?

Would you trust a mentor if you knew he was cheating on his wife?

Everyone answers these questions with a loud no! There's no way I'm giving my money to someone who steals. I will not give my trust to someone who lies. I'm not following a leader who has no moral foundation, nor will people follow you if you have no moral foundation.

This is why Paul instructed Timothy, in 1 Timothy 4:16, to guard his life closely. He knew that no one would follow Timothy if he failed morally as a leader. Beyond that, Paul knew that people would not respond to the gospel if it didn't produce true change in the lives of its leaders. This is the second part of the equation. Paul knew Timothy needed a solid foundation of doctrine so he would have something to teach. But Paul also knew the seriousness of backing up that teaching with a moral foundation. You may not consider yourself a leader, but if you have your mind set on making a difference in the world, or even in your neighborhood, school, or community, then you are a leader. To be a successful leader, you must first change yourself. The good news is that the one thing you have control over is changing yourself. You cannot control the weather, where you were born, or even how people will respond to your dream, but you can control you, including your development and growth. You can change how you respond to people, how you spend your time, and how you spend your money. You can change a lot about yourself if you are willing to.

Evaluate

Changing the world starts with laying a foundation of integrity. Take a few minutes to explore this self-inventory.

- Can people trust me?
- When I tell someone I'll do something for them, do I follow through?
- Do I lie to people?
- Do I fudge the truth to make myself look better?
- Do I show up when I tell people I will?
- Are there habits in my life I don't want people to know about?

These are just a few questions that will help you see the condition of your integrity. How you answer these questions directly affects your ability to lead a movement of change. Without a foundation, your life will crumble under the pressure of the world. Paul knew it to be true, so he instructed Timothy to guard his life.[4] Watching your life is about becoming a person people will follow.

It's about you becoming a leader.

It's about you doing the right thing for the right reasons.

It's about you being trustworthy.

It's about you leading by example.

It's about you being prepared.

It's about you being willing to sacrifice.

It's about you trusting in God when times are uncertain.

It's about you working hard, even when there's no end in sight.

Leading is about caring more for what God wants from you than people do. Watching your life will be a continual process. You will never wake up and get a pass. There are no off days. If you want to change the world, you have to lead. And leading is hard.

How to Fall from the Top of the World

When you hear on the news that a leader had an affair or a drug abuse problem, what is your first reaction? Most people are shocked and cannot believe that he or she would have done that. "He was such a nice guy," people say, or, "She seemed to have the perfect life." I know I tend to have that type of response. Part of me is shocked, then another part is sad and disappointed. Finding out the home run records in Major League in the 1990s and 2000s were due to players using illegal steroids was such a disappointment.

I grew up right outside Atlanta, Georgia. I remember as a kid pulling for the Atlanta Braves, but back in the 1980s, they were terrible. That would all change. Soon, the Braves went from worst to first and won the National League in 1991. For more than a decade, they ruled the National League. While the Braves turned things around, the other pro franchises in the city looked awfully similar to the pre-1991 Braves. The Hawks (basketball) and Falcons (football) were likewise terrible. With the exception of one season, the Falcons were hard to watch and embarrassing to pull for. But this, too, was all about to change.

In 2001, the Falcons drafted Michael Vick, one of the most athletic and gifted college quarterbacks ever. Michael came into Atlanta with high expectations and he did not disappoint. Within a few short years, Vick became a superstar in the NFL, and the Atlanta Falcons were back on the map. He became the first quarterback to throw for 2,000 yards and rush for 1,000 in the same season. He was a three-time selection to the Pro Bowl. In Atlanta, few people were as highly respected and recognized as Michael Vick.

His #7 jersey could be seen all around the city, and not just on game days.

In July 2007, all this changed. Radically. Instead of going from worst to first like the Braves, Vick took the opposite route. Details started coming out about an illegal dog-fighting ring run by gamblers at one of Vick's homes in Virginia. Reports claimed that Vick and his friends were raising dogs to fight and kill each other while people bet on the winners. By August, Vick pled guilty to hosting illegal dog fights, sharing in the profits, and providing most of the start-up financing. He admitted that he knew colleagues had killed several dogs by drowning or hanging. After this, he was released from his contract with the Falcons, lost his endorsements, filed for bankruptcy, was suspended from the NFL, and sentenced to eighteen months in a federal prison.

How could this happen? How could someone with so much throw it all away? It happened because Vick did not guard his character. He allowed those closest to him to influence him, and unfortunately they were not good influences. If you want long-term success, you need to guard your character. Going from first to worst is something you want no part of.

In your effort to change the world, you need to realize that you are entering a war zone. You will battle numerous adversaries on all sides and the toughest battle will be guarding your character. Nothing takes as long to build and is as easy to lose as character. All it takes is one mistake to sabotage everything you've worked so hard to achieve. One inappropriate phone call or remark and it's over. You must do everything in your power to guard your character.

One of the best ways to guard your character is to guard who you spend time with. Not to sound too much like your mom, but the friends you spend the most time with will affect you the most. If your best friends spend a lot of time working out and eating healthy, odds are you will, too. If your best friends spend the weekends getting drunk and eating junk food, odds are you will, too. If the people you spend the most time with trash talk their bosses, spouses, or other friends, odds are you will, too. And if your best friends spend their weekends hosting illegal dog fights, odds are you will, too. Who you spend the most time with will greatly influence you. Listen to what Solomon, the wisest man in the world, said to his son in Proverbs 1:10–16:

> My son, if sinners entice you, do not give in to them. If they say, "Come along with us; let's lie in wait for someone's blood, let's waylay some harmless soul; let's swallow them alive, like the grave, and whole, like those who go down to the pit; we will get all sorts of valuable things and fill our houses with plunder; throw in your lot with us, and we will share a common purse"—my son, do not go along with them, do not set foot on their paths; for their feet rush into sin, they are swift to shed blood.

Solomon was pleading with his son to choose his friends carefully because he knew their influence could put him on the path of destruction. He said, "Don't let them entice you." The only way a group can entice you is if you are around them. One of the best ways to avoid bad influence is to avoid those people. Do not let just anyone into your inner circle. Your inner circle is very important, and you should take great consideration on whose counsel you seek and whose opinions you trust. Now, I'm not saying you have to leave all your old friends in the dust and never talk to them again. I'm saying, if your old friends are not wise, then find some friends who are and bring them into the loop.

What do you want from an inner circle? As some of my close friends Mike and Jud say, you want someone who will stab you in the front. Stabbing you in the front means your friends will give you honest feedback, even if it hurts or is be difficult to hear. Stabbing you in the front means warning you if you are about to get on a path that leads to falling off a cliff. It also means telling you if your organization's vision has become more about you than the organization. When a friend stabs you in the front, he shows you how much he cares and respects you. Do not kick someone out of your inner circle if they stab you in the front. Those friends are rare, and you need them.

Later in Proverbs Solomon says, *"He who walks with the wise grows wise, but a companion of fools suffers harm"* (Proverbs 13:20).

A Good Bit of Advice

I got some amazing advice from a mentor a few years ago that had a huge impact on me. I was talking on the phone with him, hoping to learn about leading an organization and becoming a better leader so that I could do my part to change the world.

"So, I would love to hear your thoughts on how I can grow our organization," I said. "Specifically I could use some help when it comes to fundraising, marketing our message, and building a stronger team."

I could tell by the silence that I'd said something wrong.

He paused and then said, "Before we get into any of that, you need to figure out your non-negotiables."

"I'm not too sure what you mean," I said.

"A non-negotiable is something that, no matter the circumstances or situation, you will not compromise on. This is about figuring out who you want to be before figuring out what you want to accomplish. Figure out the type of leader you want to be, the type of husband you want to be, and the type of father you want to be."

"Could you give a few examples?" I asked him.

"Sure. Do you want to be a father who is involved with your kids? If so, then your non-negotiable would be to only travel a certain number of days a year. If a non-negotiable is to be an honest person, then decide you will never lie on your taxes."

He said all the marketing in the world can never help an organization that is led by a leader who compromises. I would offer the same advice.

Over the years, I've added some non-negotiables to my list. As a husband, I will not talk bad about my wife, cut her down, or criticize her in public. As a communicator of the gospel, I will not wing a message. I decided that I would always prepare well for any sermon. Other non-negotiables: I will not endorse anything I don't agree with simply for money, and I will tell the truth. Those are some of the non-negotiables that help determine who I am.

Some other great pre-decisions you should make include how you handle money, how you report taxes, your dating standards, and your sex life. The hardest areas of your life to constantly make the best decisions are the areas that carry the most emotion, which usually include money and relationships. Make those decisions first. Decide who you want to be, then decide what you want to accomplish.

Wisdom from Mark

This past year, I was interviewing Mark Earley, the president of Prison Fellowship, the largest prison ministry in the world, for a podcast that I host. In our time together, I asked him about how he guards his character. What are some of the steps he takes to ensure he doesn't end up on the front page of the paper for all the wrong reasons?

"Mark, we've seen recently more moral failures from high profile public leaders," I said. "Talk about how you protect yourself from that."

"For me, on a personal level, the most important thing is to recognize that I'm no different than those other examples we've seen in the media."

"Certainly that's not true," I said.

"What I mean is that on any given day, under the right set of circumstances, if I'm not careful, I could do those same thing," Mark said. "For leaders who do get themselves in trouble, it's often because when they see these moral failures in public they think they're immune from making them, too."

"So, you find ways to learn from their mistakes?" I asked.

"When I see a leader fall publicly, it has the same impact that going to a funeral does. When I go to a funeral, I'm reminded of my mortality. That's the big takeaway for me every time. And when I see these public moral failures, I'm reminded of my own propensity to sin and my own propensity to leave Jesus Christ at a whim."

"Okay. So, what is the next step then? How do we protect ourselves?" I pressed.

"I think that's the most important thing, and we have to be honest with ourselves. While we may be new creatures in Christ, or been Christians for a long time, the fact of the matter is, Satan roars like a prowling lion. And if we're not careful, we can find ourselves in a very, very vulnerable position."

"So what does this look like practically?"

"I have a weekly standing call with a friend who I share everything with. The great part is I know he has my best interest at heart."

"What about within the ministry itself?" I asked.

"At Prison Fellowship, we have on our board an accountability team," he said. "The team is made up of two or three individuals and I meet with them on a regular basis, usually by phone, because they're spread out around the country. With them I am an open book, and I have a similar trust and confidence that they have my best interest at heart."

"Can you think of a way where leaders mess that up?" I asked. "What would you suggest they do differently?"

"A leader needs to build accountability into his life. The tendency for many leaders is to build in isolation. Most leaders tend to isolate themselves. They prefer to work alone. And that puts us in a very vulnerable position."

What I loved about my time with Mark and his interview was his overwhelming since of humility. Numerous times, he said he's no different from those who fail, or that he could be that person with one poor mistake. I know I tend to think to myself, "I would never do that," or "How could he be so stupid?" Mark takes the opposite approach and reminds himself that he could easily be that guy if he is not careful. He runs one of the largest Christian parachurch ministries and, instead of boasting in his position, he remains humble. As you grow in your influence, you will have an opportunity to think you have outgrown the temptation to compromise, that you are above it. You would be wise to heed Mark's words and recognize you are not above temptation.

As a leader, do you tend to isolate yourself? Do you prefer to make decisions alone? I agree with Mark that this is a dangerous habit to get into. I'm not saying you have to hold a committee meeting every time you need to make a decision, but having a group of trusted friends, friends who know the decisions you are making *and* why you are making them, will offer loads of protection over the course of your life.

Here's a principle to keep in mind: if you don't want to tell those closest to you about a decision you are going to make, it's probably not a good decision. If you have people around you who have your best in mind, as Mark does, then it would be foolish not to get their feedback. If you have become accustomed to isolating yourself in your life and decision-making, you need to implement immediate change. The first step is to admit that to some close friends. It may be awkward or difficult at first, but it's better than ending up on the front page of the paper.

Scout

There are many signs you can look for to see how your character is going. One of the best ways is to be on the lookout for areas where you know you are prone to hide the truth from others. If you instantly think that you don't have any, then you are on to something. The process of killing your character usually starts in small ways. When someone's character explodes like a bomb, it rarely happens from one isolated event. Alcoholics don't wake up one day, have a drink, and get hooked. They usually start out drinking beer, and then move on to cocktails. After a while, that gets old and they move to the hard stuff. Stay on that path long enough and you become an addict.

The same process is at stake for your character. Rarely will someone wake up and say, "I want to embezzle $5 million dollars today." It starts with something smaller, like taking some petty cash or fudging an expense report. Add a few zeros on a mileage chart, and that IRS deduction starts to add up. After a few years, it's hard to stop. Until you get busted.

I saw this happen firsthand with a job I took a few years out of college. I was a mortgage broker and went to work for a financial planning firm that needed another representative. While there, I also received my insurance and securities licenses. It seemed like a nice place to work. The office was nicely decorated and well-equipped with the latest technological equipment. In the parking lot sat a Lexus, Volvo, BMW, and some nice SUVs. From the outside, the success was obvious.

After working a few months, I began to have questions. Certain things just didn't add up. It wasn't quite as bad as in *The Firm*, but there were some serious holes in the explanation of how things were financed. After sixteen months, I received an opportunity to work with another broker in town and decided to leave the firm. This would prove to be an amazing decision for a number of reasons.

The best reason came about a year later. I was sitting in the airport waiting on a flight to Washington, D.C., when my phone rang.

"Greg! What are you doing? Are you watching TV? Are you in front of your computer? Have you heard?"

"Sitting in the airport. No. No. And I don't think so. Heard what?"

"We now know all the answers," he said.

This was a friend I had worked with at the first firm. I hadn't spoken with him in months, so the call was somewhat out of the blue.

"Answers to what?" I asked.

"The cars. The office. The vacation homes. We know how he paid for it all."

I assumed he was referring to our old boss.

"Let me read you the headline to this news story," my friend continued. "'Local financial services company under investigation as owner cannot explain to clients where their money is.'"

"What!?!" I said loud enough for everyone in the terminal to look at me.

He continued, "It is believed that the business owner has stolen close to $5 million over the past six years in one of the largest Ponzi schemes in the state's history. It started with the owner taking a little bit of the profits from a customer's account and reporting a slightly smaller increase. Later he convinced clients to take out between $100,000 and $250,000 mortgages on their homes to invest with him. Each month he sent out fake account statements with the 'increases' or 'decreases' for each client, but it took six years for any of them to realize the money was actually sitting in someone else's checking account."

"This is unbelievable!" I said.

"So the FBI has been at the offices gathering evidence."

At that moment, all the dots were connecting in my head.

"A trial is set for a later date," he said.

"I've got to board my flight now. Let me know if you hear any-thing else," I said.

When I got home, there was a letter saying I could not destroy any paperwork, emails, or data from the time I had worked there. I had no problem with that, as I had nothing to hide.

The best way to guard against a moral failure is to watch for small inconsistencies in your character. If you get uneasy speaking about a decision you've recently made, this would be a good place to start. Over time, these small decisions will add up to big mis-takes or great accomplishments. Have someone or a small group of trusted friends with whom you can share this. Remember, it takes a long time to build a solid character and only an instant to lose it. With your character comes influence, and with influence comes your ability to change the world. Be on the lookout. Guard your character!

CHAPTER 4
REVEALING CHARACTER

*"Character is higher
than intellect."*
—RALPH WALDO EMERSON

Certainly There's Someone Else Coming

Character is not built overnight. There are no three simple steps to instant character. In the last chapter, we talked about the importance of guarding your character. But having great character is not just about defense—the guarding, protecting, and defending. It's also about the offense—being pro-active. Building character is all about pursuing the best possible decisions. When you do this, you ultimately set an example for the world to see. That is one way to look at your effectiveness—are you setting the right example?

When I was in high school, I spent a summer working for a carpenter trying to save money for college. We did a little bit of everything: carpentry, sheetrock, trim, cabinetry, and painting. Painting was the one area where I actually had a good bit of experience. My grandfather ran his own paint contracting company for four decades, and whenever I needed some extra cash growing up, I could go and "work" a couple of days for him.

One morning I showed up to work for the carpenter and he said, "Grab those paint cans, the brush, and dropcloths and head to this address."

I grabbed the piece of paper out of his hand. "What am I doing?" I asked.

"Painting the trim in her kitchen. Should be a pretty easy job," he said.

I threw the stuff in my car and headed over, arriving around 7:30. I will never forget the look on her face as she opened the door to let me in.

"Can I help you?" she said. She looked me up and down and, if it wasn't for the bucket of paint and some brushes, there was no way in the world she would have thought *I* was there to do the painting.

My first few thoughts were a bit sarcastic. *Well, I'm here to return these paint supplies I found in your driveway. Yeah, you can help me; let me in so I can do my job.*

"I'm here to paint the kitchen," I said. Awkward pause.

"Okay," she said as she opened the door.

She reluctantly let me in, and I went about my business. I should tell you that I really did know what I was doing. I had plenty of experience and was very particular about detailed work like painting. All she saw was a teenage kid. She didn't see years of experience. Around lunchtime, I heard the phone ring.

"Yes. He's here… It's taking a little longer than I thought… Well, yes. He's doing a fine job… it looks great."

She was obviously talking to my boss. She said something about my age. I found out later that my boss asked her if I was doing a good job, and when she said yes, he asked exactly what the problem was. If he's doing a good job, then it doesn't matter how old he is, does it?

That story brings up two feelings for me as I look back. The first one is annoyance. It was flat-out annoying the way I was looked up and down and considered too young to be able to do a good job. The second feeling is pride. Knowing that I did do a good job and that she was pleased after I finished gave me the satisfaction of realizing what I was capable of.

As I've gotten older, though, I can look back on that experience and understand why I was questioned at the front door that day. You see, for the most part, young people have set the bar very low… and we live up to those low standards perfectly. When people find out you are doing something about it, they will assume you are not up to the task. They don't expect you to chase a dream. They expect you to go to college, get a good job, work forty hours a week, get married, have 2.5 kids, and live in the suburbs. When they find out you are working in the inner city or going overseas, they won't get it. And many times, they'll just look down on you, just like the lady at the door looked down on me. But don't let that stop you—you have to rise above it.

This same problem was evident in the first century when Paul addressed his young friend Timothy. Paul's official charge to Timothy, in 1 Timothy 4:12, was how to live (act, behave) in order to change his world. Paul saw in Timothy a great ability to make a huge impact on the world, but he also knew that many others would just see a punk kid who talked too much. To overcome that, Paul pointed out five key areas in which Timothy was to stand out and be different. These areas make up your character.

Paul began with this statement to Timothy: *"Don't let anyone look down on you because you are young..."* (1 Timothy 4:12). Paul told him not to get down on himself when he got to the door and they expected someone older, more experienced, or with more credentials. Don't let them get to you, he said. But beyond encouragement, Paul also issued a warning. Another way to look at this is to say, "Do not give them a reason to look down on you..." Paul knew that unless Timothy's lifestyle matched his words, Timothy's message of the gospel would lose all authority. He'd be dead in the water. In the same verse, Paul continued and said, *"...but set an example for the believers..."* Paul told Timothy to show the way. Set the example. Light the path. Be the person who others look to, to know how to act. Paul then gave specific examples of how Timothy was supposed to set the example. Let's look at each one and their implications for us.

In Speech...

What you talk about and how you talk about it reveals a great deal about who you really are. Have you ever been around someone who just loved to talk about themselves? They talk about their education achievements as if they're the smartest person alive, or they relive their glory days when they hit the game-winning shot. They love to be the center of the conversation. It's evident from a few minutes of conversation that the most important person in his life is him.

Have you ever been around a family that is extremely passionate about a particular cause? I knew a guy who was the most extreme health freak when it came to food and diet. He literally ate the weirdest foods, most of which I'd never even heard of. He told me that he didn't like to take his family to visit his parents because it was too much of a burden on their diet. In fact, he was considering home-schooling his kids because of the weird foods his kids ate. He was afraid they'd get made fun of! He used to talk about organic this and all-natural that. One thing was for sure—I never doubted how serious he was about his health.

What we talk about is the first sign revealing what we care about. It also shows the level of significance. This is why setting an example in speech is so important. It's the first impression people get from you. What you talk about matters. As does what you joke about, who you talk about, and how you talk about them. If all your friends are making fun of another individual, you have two options, and both involve setting an example. You can join in and show that you are no different from anyone else there, or you can choose not to and set a better example.

Let's look at the jokes we like to tell or laugh at. Do we tell jokes that ridicule another person based upon race, gender, age, or where they live? Do we make fun of developmentally-delayed people or those with disabilities? Do we joke about having affairs or other inappropriate things we'd like to do with some other person? By the way, fewer things irk me more than hearing husbands talking about what they wish they could do to that girl who is not their wife. Do they not understand that they are joking about adultery? I just don't understand the humor in that. And while I'm on the topic, even if you are just dating someone, have a decent level of commitment to the person you're dating and don't joke about that. If that's what you do while you're dating, then odds are you will continue the practice when you are married. By saying these things, we are setting an example, but not one that will make any difference in the world. Choose your words wisely; they reveal what is truly in your heart.

In Life...

The next topic that Paul talks about is setting an example in life. To put it another way, this is the way you behave. This is a broad call, covering everything from how you spend your money to the people you spend time with. It includes how you dress and the words you use. It incorporates the details of each day and the broad vision you have for your career and family. Setting an example in *life* is about your daily decisions. This is important to those who are around us each day. If we are committed to changing the world, it will happen by taking consistent actions over a very long period. Setting an example with your life is not a one-time event. Because you give a homeless person five bucks one day does not mean you are committed to loving the least of these. Passing on alcohol when you are underage one time means nothing if the next week you are passed out on the floor. Being sexually pure in your dating relationship for the first six months is not setting an example if you start sleeping with each other because you have moved into a "committed relationship." This idea of setting an example in life is a commitment to long-term growth and action.

Going back to my hero, William Wilberforce tried for twenty consecutive years to abolish the slave trade in the British Parliament before he actually made it happen. What would have happened if, after the first or second year he was voted down, he said, "Well, I tried, and it just isn't going to happen"? Would we really look back on his life as one of the most committed abolitionists in history? No. We wouldn't, because it took a commitment longer than two years. This is what Paul is telling you. Setting an example with your life is not a one-time transaction; it is a yearly, monthly, daily, and even hourly commitment. And this is the requirement for changing the world.

In Love...

The next area where Paul instructs Timothy to set an example is in love. This can be seen in how we treat people. Most Jews at the time of Christ had an understanding of what it meant to love people. They were supposed to love their friends and hate their enemies. Remember the whole eye-for-an eye thing? Well, when Jesus came along, he blew the expectations of love out of the water. Listen to how he raised the bar when it comes to loving people.

> You have heard that it was said, "Love your neighbor and hate your enemy." But I tell you: Love your enemies and pray for those who persecute you, that you may be sons of your Father in heaven. He causes the sun to rise on the evil and the good, and sends rain on the righteous and the unrighteous. If you love those who love you, what reward will you get? Are not even the tax collectors doing that? And if you greet only your brothers, what are you doing more than others? Do not even pagans do that? Be perfect,

therefore, as your heavenly Father is perfect.
(Matthew 5:43–48)

This was so drastically different for the Jews, but looking at it from a we-want-to-change-the-world viewpoint, it just seems so logical. Jesus is basically asking, "How in the heck are you going to differentiate yourselves from the pagans, the non-religious, the heathens, and the non-believers if you just act the same way they do?"

But you say—and they probably did, too—"We don't *act* like them. We don't go to *those parties*. We don't *watch that*. We don't *buy that*." That may very well be true, but Jesus is taking it to another level. The bar has been raised. He says that if you only love those who love you, you are no different from the heathen. If you are nice to only those who are nice to you, you are like the pagan. If you respect those who respect you, you are just like the non-believer who does not have the truth of Christ in him. Jesus says we must love those who persecute us. We must pray for those who hate us. We must love people even if they do not love us. The bar has been raised.

I'm going to be honest with you; this is probably the hardest command in all of Scripture. Like many commands of Jesus, this is not logical. It makes sense to love those who love you, to give to those who give to you, to be nice to those who are nice to you. But to do that for someone who is a complete jerk is not intuitive. This is a major distinguishing mark of a Christian, and a prerequisite if you want to radically change the world. One reason this is distinguishably Christian is that only through the love of Christ and the power of the Holy Spirit can someone continually love an enemy. Jesus was able to do this as he was hanging on the cross while the

Romans, and even the criminal beside him, continued to mock and ridicule him. By loving these people, he set himself apart from every teacher, prophet, and leader in history. As the ultimate example, he now calls us to do the same. Paul recognized the power of this principle and encouraged Timothy to set the example in love.

In Faith...

The next command from Paul is to set the example of faith. This is how we trust God. Whether or not you realize this, when you became a Christian, people begin to watch you. They want to see if your new claim of faith is real. They watch to see if you will actually live out what you claim to believe.

Practically, it looks like this: when you feel God leading you to a certain college but you don't know how to pay for it, will you trust God and go anyway? You believe you are called to a life of purity, so will you stop sleeping with your boyfriend or girlfriend and trust that God's way will be more fulfilling? If you lose a loved one unexpectedly, will you trust God in your mourning, or will you become bitter or angry? If you do not make the team or sport you tried out for, will you degrade the other players behind their back by telling everyone you should have been picked, or will you love your enemies? When you know God is leading you to transfer to a different city, will you be obedient even though it means leaving friends and family behind? When you are offered a job that pays really well but you know you shouldn't take it, will you trust God for provision? Setting an example of faith means choosing to trust God in uncertain times. It means sticking with his plan even when it gets difficult. It means staying committed to his principles even when everyone around you cuts corners.

As I mentioned before, during my first year of marriage I took a job with a mortgage brokerage selling loans. The previous five years of my life had been in some sort of ministry. This was before the mortgage crisis of 2008, so the lending laws were very different than they are now. When I started work, the industry was coming down the mountain of unprecedented growth in the industry. Companies were making a lot of money. Looking back, we see that much of it had to do with shady lending policies. Because of the recent history of profits and sales, the pressure to produce (i.e. sell mortgages and other loans) was almost unrealistic.

I really shot myself in the foot because, during my first month there, I sold a mortgage which my co-workers said usually takes people four to six months to do. After about six months, we got a new manager who was ready to prove himself as a sales leader and large producer. I had a stretch of time where I wasn't selling a lot. We were supposed to sell a certain number of loans a month, but also had to make a certain number of calls per day. If we didn't hit those daily numbers, we did not have much leverage when it came to lack of production. I was told that if I didn't start hitting higher numbers, my job would be in danger. That's never a good feeling.

At about the same time, two opportunities came my way. The first was from a co-worker who weeks before had been given a similar warning about his numbers. He came to me one day and said he had something that could help me out. He showed me a way to doctor my numbers in the system so that it looked like I was doing more than I actually was. I was staring down unemployment, and it seemed as if a perfect opportunity had fallen into my lap.

The second opportunity came the next day, when my new boss heard me on the phone trying to make a sale. When I was done, he asked me to come to his desk and listen to how he made a sales call. He was going to show me the secret for selling this particular product. "Just tell them we're running a special for clients like them for this month only and that they will save thousands of dollars in fees and other expenses if they get the loan now." Well, here was the problem: that particular product didn't have any of the fees he was talking about. Ever. They simply did not exist. So, while technically he was right in saying there were no fees that month, he was deceiving the clients into thinking they were getting a special deal. In other words, he wanted me to lie to the client.

That was a tough season of life. I was under pressure to provide for my family. Each day when I walked into work I felt the pressure to perform. There was the pressure to lie about my numbers. Then there was the pressure from the boss to deceive clients to make the sale. I would sit there and not know if what I was being told to do was ethical.

Looking back, I am glad to say that in both cases I decided I was not going to accept the offer, no matter what the consequences were. It came down to the question, do I trust God more than I trust my circumstances? Do I trust that, if I work hard and do not cheat the system, God will honor me? In other words, do I have the faith to believe that ultimately God is in charge, not the new hotshot boss? The next few months were still extremely rough. Each day I had to go to work not knowing whether or not it would be my last. I was constantly pressured about my numbers, but I kept doing my job the best I knew how. It was a great feeling to walk in that last day and give my resignation letter.

You will have similar opportunities to make decisions that will allow you to set an example in faith. Others will see how you act in those uncertain situations. It will also give you an opportunity to grow your own faith and have a milestone to look back on. God showed himself faithful in providing for my family, and I will always have that to build upon when making future decisions. Set an example in your faith, in the way you trust God.

In Purity…

The last area Paul commanded Timothy to be different and to set the example was in purity. Despite the current notion that purity deals only with the physical, purity in its purist sense is actually all about the heart. All of our physical impurity has its birth in our hearts. Impurity with our eyes comes from lust in the heart. Impurity with our mouths comes from anger in our hearts. Impurity with our money comes from greed in our hearts.

Impurity's starting line is actually in our heart. Listen to how Jesus described this process in Luke 6: *"No good tree bears bad fruit, nor does a bad tree bear good fruit"* (Luke 6:43). In other words, a pure heart does not reveal impurity, nor does an impure heart reveal purity. If your heart is pure, your actions will flow from that purity. Jesus went on to say, *"The good man brings good things out of the good stored up in his heart, and the evil man brings evil things out of the evil stored up in his heart. For out of the overflow of his heart his mouth speaks"* (Luke 6:45). So this becomes the basis for purity. But why is this important? Why make such a big deal about it? In the famous Sermon on the Mount, Jesus taught the crowds and told them, *"Blessed are the pure in heart, for they will see God"* (Matthew 5:8).

Wow! Did you catch that? Jesus is saying that if we are pure in heart, we will actually see God. Now, I don't necessarily think that means we'll see him with our eyes right now. I think it means we'll be able to hear what he's saying to us, learn what he's teaching us, and obey what he's telling us to do. And isn't this what we ultimately want? Don't we want to have the full confidence of knowing what God is calling us to? I know I do. I want to know the path I'm walking down is his chosen path for me. I want to be at peace about the decisions I am making for my present and future. I want to hear his voice. I want to see him. The only way that can happen is when I am pure in heart.

David shows us the same truth hundreds of years earlier in the Psalms. He wrote, *"Who may ascend the hill of the Lord? Who may stand in his holy place?"* (Psalms 24:3) In other words, who may come near to God? Who can be in his presence? Who can hear his voice and worship him? The answer to David's question is going to sound very similar: *"He who has clean hands and a pure heart, who does not lift his soul to an idol or swear by what is false"* (Psalms 24:4). If you didn't catch that the first time, read it again. A pure heart leads to seeing, hearing, and worshiping God! If you have a pure heart, you can hear God.

Earlier we saw that Paul wants us to set an example with our faith. We said that faith is trusting that what God has for me will be far greater than what I can get on my own. In my experience, the enemy twists this truth more than any other to get people to fall into impurity, especially sexual impurity. Remember, God desires for us to be pure so we can see him. God says that saving yourself sexually for marriage will be far greater than having sex now. The enemy says, "No, it will be greater to have sex now *and* when you get married." In the moment, we have thoughts like, *It seems right.*

*We're in love. She's the person I've been waiting for. He'll be disap-
pointed if we don't.* There are a thousand other lies floating between your mind, your heart, and the other parts of your body. But
the question here is this: do you truly believe that what God has
for you is greater than what you can get for yourself?

Primetime TV is not talking about how your sexual past will
affect your marriage. Hollywood is not concerned about the emo-
tional fear it brings into your relationship with your new spouse.
None of your single friends who are hooking up can tell you how
those decisions will affect your future.

Setting the example in purity is so important because it is the
way that we see God. When we are impure, we impede our ability
to hear his voice, know his will, and follow his call. If we set a bad
example with this, we impede others' ability to hear his voice,
know his will, and follow his call. We must make wise decisions
about our purity. Deciding beforehand will help you greatly in
your quest for purity. We must believe that what God has for us in
the future is greater than what we can get for ourselves now.

It All Starts Here

It all starts with you. If you want to change the world, you have to
change yourself. Changing the world is about leading people, and
they will not follow you unless you are worth following. You become worth following when you set the example of faith, when
you don't back down to criticism, and when you persevere, even
when it's easier to quit.

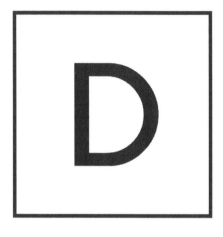

DOCTRINE

CHAPTER 5
YOUR ANCHOR

*"Therefore everyone who hears these words of mine and
puts them into practice is like a wise man who built his
house on the rock. The rain came down, the streams rose,
and the wind blew and beat against that house; yet it did
not fall, because it had its foundation on the rock."*
—JESUS CHRIST
(MATTHEW 7:24–25)

What You Believe Matters

What you believe determines what you think, and what
you think determines what you do, and what you do
will determine if you change the world. Having a
solid character allows you to get others involved and lead them in
creating change. Your character guides you during tough deci-

sions, but your beliefs will give you the hope to keep fighting. Belief matters.

A few generations ago, belief went by another word—doctrine. But somewhere in the past few decades, doctrine became disassociated with belief and branded with boring. Talking about doctrine meant putting people to sleep on pews. (Remember those?) Discussing the philosophical tenants of faith is boring and bothers most Christians today. Why? Because we want to see faith in action. One group says it this way, "Give us deeds, not creeds." Many of you connect with that idea immediately, which is why you've decided to do something about it. You are putting your faith into action. You are taking the call to love your neighbor seriously. You are looking after the widow, orphan, and alien. Deeds not creeds, right? Not if you want long-term success. One of my heroes said this in response to "deeds over creeds." He said, "If it wasn't for the creed, I wouldn't do the deed."

So what's the point in having a solid doctrine? Will it really make a difference in my attempt to do something about it? The answer is an overwhelming yes. There are numerous reasons doctrine will help you in your attempt to change the world. One reason is that having a solid doctrinal foundation will give you the motivation to do something about it.

Behind Bars

In 1973, the total prison population in the United States was around 150,000 inmates. By 1980, that numbered doubled to 305,000. Since then, there has been a 500 percent increase to more than two million inmates in 2009. These statistics are disturbing and overwhelming.

But one man decided to do something about it. After being sentenced to prison for his involvement with Watergate, Chuck Colson, former aide to President Richard Nixon, saw firsthand the issues facing the prison system and culture at large. The current system was not working to prevent crime or reform criminals. For the next thirty-five years, Colson set out to make a difference in the justice system in America and around the world. Facing opposition from governments and lobbyists, Colson persevered for decades because he was anchored in his beliefs and had a foundation built on biblical truth. In fact, it was his study of Scripture where he found the catalyst of his new life purpose. It was this sense of biblical justice that started him down the path to do something about the justice system. For Chuck, if it hadn't been for the creeds he wouldn't have done the deeds.

I had the opportunity to talk with Chuck about his journey. Some key areas of interest are how biblical doctrine guided him in his decisions and convictions. Biblical truth was literally his proof that he had to do something about the prisons. Today, millions of lives have been impacted by Chuck's willingness to do something about it. He literally changed the world.

On July 9, 1974, Colson began a one- to three-year prison sentence for obstruction of justice on charges not directly linked to the Watergate scandal. After serving seven months at Maxwell Correctional Facility in Alabama, Colson was released. His goal was to begin practicing law again and to try moving on from the scandal. This plan never quite panned out as he thought.

"What was it like when you were released from prison?" I asked him.

"When I got out in 1975, I was absolutely shocked by the conditions, problems, and lack of rehabilitation I saw in that prison. The people were absolutely helpless and hopeless. Literally, men would lie in bunks and stare into emptiness all day. They were just bodies atrophying and souls corroding."

"What was your next move? Did you have big plans for a prison ministry?"

"I didn't want to go into ministry," he said. "I planned on going back into law. I tried to think of ways that I might be able to help the prison system out. I wrestled with it."

"So what changed your mind?"

"God gave me a call to go to into the prisons. It was very clear. It was not something I wanted. It was certainly not something my wife wanted. But once I felt certain of that, we organized a ministry on a shoestring and the royalties of my first book, *Born Again*, and we started going into the prisons."

"What was your goal when you went into the prisons?"

"I have a passion for justice and wanting to see the justice system work properly," he explained. "I wanted to see it do what it's supposed to do, which is restore order to the community and punish where necessary. But the system was a giant therapeutic attempt to take people out of their unfortunate environments and put them into a place where they could become penitent, hence the word penitentiary. Or where they could become reformed, hence reformatory. And I saw what a complete failure it was."

He continued, "Previous research said that prisoners were victims because they lived in poverty or bad environments. In other words, it was not their fault they committed crimes. If this was the case, why does the wealthiest nation on the planet have one of the highest incarceration rates? In the mid-1970s, two doctors did a seventeen-year-long study in Washington of the inmate population and came to a conclusion that startled them because they had

started out with the same presupposition. They discovered that
crime is not caused by poverty but by wrong moral choices. They
said, 'The answer to crime is the conversion of the offender to a
more responsible lifestyle.' Another study, done later at Harvard in
1986, said that crime is caused by a lack of moral training in the
morally formative years."

"So what effect did this new research have on you?"

"When I read that particular study, light bulbs went off, and I
said to myself, 'The problem I'm trying to deal with, of bringing
justice into the prisons and rehabilitate inmates, one of the biggest
social problems we have in America, is never going to be dealt with
while the prevailing worldview we live by in America is so skewed.'
People are being told to live only for themselves, and they're told
they're not responsible for their behavior, and I could see that this
was really a deeper issue than just the prisons. I began to see that
the real cause of crime and social decay in our country was from
people having a flawed view of what their responsibilities are in
life. Their worldview is flawed.

"What do you mean, worldview? What determines one's
worldview?" I asked.

"There are four critical questions that determine all world-
views. 1) Where did we come from? 2) Why is there sin and suffering? 3) Is there a way out? 4) What's my purpose? How you answer those questions determines everything. And I could see that
Americans were answering those questions improperly. Evolution
had begun to really take over in the schools, and in the sixties you
had a whole movement that was trying to take us away from our
traditional understanding of God."

"How do the worldview questions and the prisons connect?
What's the connection for us?"

"I've found the strongest churches in prisons, because they really understand sin and they really understand redemption in a way that most people in churches do not. If you look at those four questions, I believe that only Christianity answers them logically. This is the big missing ingredient in the church today. I think this is why people are hungry and looking for something else. They're looking to find something that will give real meaning to their Christian experience. And if it's just a relationship with Jesus and your sins are forgiven—that's a wonderful thing. But then you go back to church week after week and you hear the same things, you do your Bible studies, and you begin to wonder, 'What more is there in all this? How does this relate to what's going on in the world today?'"

"There has definitely been a shift in younger Christians towards action," I agreed. "Social justice causes have become the battle cry of younger evangelicals. What do you think about that?"

"I find younger Evangelicals are asking the right questions: What's the church really supposed to do? Why are we sitting here Sunday after Sunday? Is this just a conversation we have with one another, or is there something more? Is this objectively real? Is it true? Can it be proven? How do I put my faith into action?

"The great thing about the Christian worldview is that once you have been redeemed, you have been saved from your sins," he continued. "But you have been saved with a purpose, and that purpose is to glorify God with your life. And I don't care whether you are a carpenter, business executive, solider, or a minister—you have a ministry to do for Christ everyday because you are trying to live out your worldview in the marketplace, trying to bring Christian truth into every area of life. So that's why, after my work in the prisons, I saw that the real failure in society is much less political, much less structural, much less systemic—it is really a public problem with the terms of public attitude. It's really an abandonment of the historic *anchor* we had with moral restraints with a biblical understanding of life."

"What then is the key to seeing real change? How can people change culture and the world?"

"The answer is, if you are going to change anything, you start by changing yourselves. Then you change the church, and ground yourselves in biblical truth as it relates to all life and how you then winsomely defend that and, more importantly, how you winsomely live that out in your day-to-day life. Christians need to be grounded biblically. It starts there."

Read that again. To change anything, you start by changing yourself and then grounding yourself in biblical truth. It was learning the doctrine of Scripture that took Chuck Colson back into the prisons to fight for true justice. It was his belief in the truths of Christianity that gave him endurance to work for more than thirty-five years to bring about change. Because of the creeds, he did the deeds.

Never Let Go

A few years ago, worship leader Matt Redman released a song that had a pretty catchy tune and was easy to sing along to. Many churches began to sing it, including the one I attended. The song was called *Never Let Go*.

Maybe you've heard the song. You may have even sung it before. It was probably a year or so after I was familiar with the song that I heard Matt talk about why he wrote it. I hadn't put much thought into why he wrote the song other than that the words sounded right and the tune was nice.

Here was his reason. On July 7, 2005, terrorists set off three bombs on the London subway system and a fourth on a double-decker bus in Tavistock Square. A total of 56 people were killed, including all four terrorists. More than 700 more people were injured. That same week, Matt's wife Beth had a miscarriage. They were living in London at the time, and as BBC One and ITV1 ran uninterrupted news coverage of the terrorist attack, Matt was filled with grief. But also hope. The words of the song were like a prayer that Matt could cling to during this time of suffering—"Through the calm and through the storm." The storm had struck close to home, and he needed something more than just a feeling to get him through. He needed something solid. He needed hope.

Hope comes from having solid doctrine. Today we hear people use the word all the time with expressions like, "I hope I get that raise," or "I hope I get that game for my birthday," or "I hope my team wins today." In this way, hope means nothing more than to wish for something. What you really mean is, "I wish I could get that raise," or "I wish I could get that game for my birthday," or "I wish my team could win today." To hope is not to wish. In a biblical context, hope in something has more to do with faith than anything. When Paul writes that our hope is secure in Christ, he isn't saying that our wish is in Christ—he's saying that we have a secure future in Christ.

Hope is like a bank. You put money in a bank and trust that it will be there in the future when you need it. Having hope is like banking on the promises that God has laid out in Scripture, knowing that they will all come to fruition at the appointed time. This idea is so important because when you face struggles or challenges, you need to know that your faith and hope have not failed you, nor has God failed you. Through those trials, God is still there; he is still sovereign, and he is still all-knowing, all-powerful, and all-loving. In those times, God is still in control. When your hope is secure, you can rest in that truth and keep fighting, keep pushing, and continue your quest to change the world.

When the Storms Come

If you have a house on the eastern coast of the United States or on the Gulf of Mexico, then the late summer and early months of fall can be incredibly nerve-wracking—for that is hurricane season. During these months, you watch the Weather Channel to see if Alvin, Bubba, or Cindy is headed your way. Seeing the spinning storms on the radar screen is your worst nightmare. Over the past few years, we've seen the devastating effects of hurricanes making landfall. When that happens, your only hope for survival is to have a secure foundation.

A few years ago, my wife and I got to go on an unbelievable trip with her parents to South America. Since her spring break was in March, we were able to get offseason prices for our trip. Combine a great deal with an amazing destination and you have the makings of a perfect vacation.

Part of our trip was taking a cruise ship around Cape Horn, the southern tip of South America. The original itinerary scheduled us to pass by the cape around mid-afternoon so that the tip would be visible. As we were heading out that morning, the captain said that the winds were really picking up around the cape, which might put us a little behind schedule. What he really meant was that the wind was blowing so hard it was going to take an extra five hours to get there! By the time the sun went down, the boat was really starting to rock. It was entertaining to sit at dinner and watch all the people trying to eat their food as their plates kept changed direction in front of them.

After we finished our meal, the captain said over the loud-speaker that we would be passing by the cape in a few minutes if we wanted to look out the starboard side—that's the right side, if you're facing forward. He also warned us that it was very windy and to be careful if we went on the deck. My father-in-law and I decided to take a chance on the deck and headed for the door. He got there first, and I thought he was going to push the door open and walk outside. Yet, he walked into the door, and it did not move. He always pulls jokes like that, so I ran into the back of him. He looked at me and said, "I'm not joking. I can't open the door." So we both started pushing on the door, and he *wasn't* joking. The wind was blowing so hard outside that it took both of us pushing to get it open. We were told that the southern point of the cape had a blinking red light on the tip if we looked out to our right. In the rain, wind, and complete darkness, we tried for ten minutes to get a picture of the elusive red light, with no luck. It was the windiest experience of my life. The next morning, the captain apologized that we missed passing the horn in the daytime, but the winds were gusting at 100 kilometers per hour!

If you spend enough time at sea, then inevitably the storms will come. That is the reality of sailing. The same is true of life, and especially of your venture to change the world. You will hit storms. They come in all shapes and sizes. Every great world changer in history faced his or her own storms. You will be no different. Your goal is not to avoid the storms; rather, your goal is to have a solid foundation to make sure you're still standing when the storm subsides.

Rock Solid

The first part of a solid foundation is your character. Without that, you cannot lead long enough to make the change you desire. The second part of a solid foundation is your doctrine, or your beliefs. I will use those terms interchangeably from now on. Paul instructed Timothy to guard his life (character) and his doctrine (beliefs). The first part seems obvious, but why doctrine? Our doctrine gives us an anchor to weather the storms. The first way this happens is by knowing that the storms will come. If we do not know our beliefs, we have unrealistic and unmet expectations. We assume God will act in a certain way, and when he doesn't there's a solid chance we'll walk away before we complete the task he's given us.

Matthew and Luke both record a sermon Jesus gave in the early part of his ministry. Matthew's version is longer and is historically called the Sermon on the Mount. In this sermon, Jesus teaches on almost every topic under the sun. He hits money, sex, relationships, prayer, worship, purpose, forgiveness, love, and work; he pretty much covered it all. After he finished teaching, he closed with this promise. Jesus said that the man who hears the words he has spoken *and* puts them into practice is incredibly wise.

> He is like a man building a house, who dug down deep and laid the foundation on rock. When a flood came, the torrent struck that house but

could not shake it, because it was well built.
(Luke 6:48)

Matthew records it like this:

> The rain came down, the streams rose, and the
> winds blew and beat against that house; yet it did
> not fall, because it had its foundation on the rock.
> (Matthew 7:25)

We learn two important points from these passages. The first
is that Jesus says storms will come. In other words, life will not
always go the way we want or plan for it to. If you believe nothing
bad will happen to you when you set out to pursue a God-given
dream, you need to reread Jesus' words. Thinking you've got a
stress-free road ahead is a false, unrealistic expectation, and a dangerous assumption. In the last hours of Jesus' ministry before he
was crucified, he told his disciples that they would have trouble in
this world, but to take heart because he had overcome the world
(John 16:33). So you need to understand that there will be trouble, heartache, tough roads, frustration, and doubt during your
journey.

The good news is that there is a second lesson we learn from
Jesus' closing promise. If you dig down deep and build your house
with a secure foundation, when the storms come there may be
some damage, but your house will be secure. Jesus said the man
who hears his words and puts them into practice would survive the
storm. This is why knowing doctrine is so crucial. Having false
doctrine will lead to poor thinking, which leads to poor decisions.
If you believe that once you pursue your idea to change the world
nothing bad will happen along the way, that poor thinking will lead

to poor decisions, which will eventually wreck your ability to complete your task. Not knowing what you believe has the same consequences. Jesus warns those that do nothing with these words:

> But the one who hears my words and does not put them into practice is like a man who built a house on the ground without a foundation. The moment the torrent struck that house, it collapsed and its destruction was complete. (Luke 6:49)

More Questions than Answers

One of the biggest misconceptions about being a Christian is that once you start to follow Christ, life gets easier, with fewer obstacles and less heartache. Many times this belief is multiplied when you attempt something big for God. I know I've fallen into this thinking before. My thoughts go something like this: *Okay God, I've decided to launch that new ministry that will help those suffering from major injustice. Since I'm doing that, everything should come together nice and easy, with no complications. I should be able to raise enough money without problems.*

Then, a few months in, I ask questions like these: *Why haven't more people helped? Why didn't the legal paperwork go through the first time? I thought if I quit my job to start this you'd provide the same salary I had at my other job. Why is this taking so much longer? Why did that group reject our proposal? Why is this harder than I thought? Why? Why? Why?*

This can be an extremely frustrating place to be. There is nothing more straining on a relationship than unmet expecta-

tions—that is, except unmet, unrealistic expectations. Having unmet, unrealistic expectations is dangerous and unhealthy for any
relationship, but especially for your relationship with God. I
thought that if I started a ministry to serve others all my requests
would work out just as I planned. I thought that in my attempt to
change the world, everything would work out perfectly. When it
became obvious that wasn't the case, I began to get frustrated and
even doubt my calling. It was a dangerous place to be. But where
did I go wrong? Did I start the ministry at the wrong time? Did I
not work hard enough? No, the problem lay in my unrealistic expectations. I needed an anchor.

When we have unrealistic expectations of God, it puts him in a
rather awkward position. We go into the day thinking that events
are guaranteed to work out a certain way, but God knows this is
not his plan. He knows the outcome will be different than we expect. We presumed one thing and then were disappointed. Then
we blame God. What is God to do? If only he could communicate
to us that life doesn't always work out the way we expect it to,
maybe we wouldn't be so disappointed when things don't work
out the way we think they should. The good news is that he already has. He left us the Bible. By knowing the Word and being
grounded in its truth, we are enabled to understand God in a
greater capacity.

Perseverance

Changing the world takes a long time. Colson has been working
for more than thirty-five years and into his seventies to change the
justice system. Mother Teresa worked in the slums of Calcutta for
half her life. The Apostle Paul endured beatings, prison, starvation,

and other persecutions for the sake of planting churches. For all of
them, it was hard work that took a long time.

That is not a popular thing to say in our world today. Something that takes a long time is old, outdated, and boring. Thanks to
fast food, microwaves, jets, cell phones, the Internet, and whatever
newest technology is around the corner, we live in a world that
wants it now. Waiting is not something our generation does well.
People didn't like waiting for their pizza to cook, so Little Caesars
introduced Hot-N-Ready Pizza, ready when you walk in the door.
People didn't like waiting for their rental car, so Enterprise picks
them up. No one likes waiting. And waiting is probably the biggest
reason that so few people change the world.

The old saying "It's worth the wait" doesn't mean much anymore, because so few people actually work on something long
enough to be able to say that. The bigger the impact you want to
make, the longer it will take to achieve. The larger the vision, the
longer the journey will be. Given this, throughout your journey
you will have multiple opportunities to quit. You will face opposition. Your donations will dry up. Your best team member will
leave. You will be told it won't work, that it can never be done, or
that you're too young. Paul told us that we would face persecution.
Unless you are rooted in the truth of the Bible, you will quit.

The truth of the Scriptures tells us that God is sovereign, that
he is in control, and that nothing happens without his knowledge.
Paul writes in Colossians that, *"He is before all things, and in him all
things hold together"* (Colossians 1:17). That is a truth we all have
to rest on, especially when times get tough. And times will get
tough. If we truly trust in God with the vision and calling he has
given, we will be able to persevere. In fact, James tells us that we
are not complete in our faith until we've persevered. He said we

should not run from an opportunity to persevere, but to view it as a blessing from God. Here's what he wrote to a group of Christians who were being persecuted for their faith in the first century:

> Consider it pure joy, my brothers, whenever you face trials of many kinds, because you know that the testing of your faith develops perseverance. Perseverance must finish its work so that you may be mature and complete, not lacking anything. (James 1:2–4)

Perseverance is something William Wilberforce should be forever praised for. As we have already seen, he fought for more than twenty years to make the world a better place by ending the British slave trade. Friends and family shunned him. His life was threatened on numerous occasions. He was voted down nineteen straight years in Parliament. On one occasion, he went to Parliament ready to vote on a bill for abolition and was excited because this time he had enough commitments from friends to make it happen. When the time came for the vote, half of his friends were absent. It turns out they'd all received free tickets to the theatre that evening from a thoughtful pro-slavery supporter. Wilberforce didn't have enough votes to pass the bill. He was lied to, deceived, and ridiculed for his "love of the negro." But none of this stopped him from finishing the task God had given him. He was able to persevere because of his faith in God, which came from his superb knowledge of the Word of God. Wilberforce was known on some occasions to spend eight hours of day in study and prayer. He knew that his ability to persevere was directly tied to his knowledge of the truth and so will yours. There is no replacement for knowing the Word. Having a foundation comes from knowing and living the truths found in the Scriptures.

COMMITMENT

CHAPTER 6
PREPARATION IS NECESSARY

*"Opportunity is missed by most
people because it is dressed in
overalls and looks like work."*
—THOMAS EDISON

The Road Less Taken

Most Olympic athletes dedicate years of their lives training to win a medal. They wake up at 4:45 am and head to the gym. After eating a bowl of oatmeal for breakfast, they complete a stretching routine for thirty minutes, followed by two hours of cardio training. From 8:00 a.m. to noon, they are working on their next routine. After a quick lunch, they head to the weight room for one hour of lifting. For those still in school, 2:00-4:00 p.m. is spent with a tutor studying and completing any class work due that week. Another two hours is spent practicing the routine, then an hour of cool down, stretching, it's time to head home. After dinner, most athletes are in bed by 9:00 p.m. ready to do it again the next morning.

This is not an uncommon routine for an athlete training for the Olympics. Most competitors will follow this routine for four to six years in their quest to claim a gold medal. While most teenagers are sleeping in on weekends and playing video games after school, Olympic athletes commit to a grueling schedule in pursuit of their dream. Olympic athletes don't just show up and expect to win. They prepare years in advance for their opportunity.

We've said that the first step in changing the world is gaining your passion for it. Then you need to have the character that allows you to lead the effort. Next, we said that you need the foundation of beliefs to withstand the trials and temptations that come up along the way.

The fourth and final element to changing the world is commitment. Commitment includes time, effort, and dedication. It takes time to do anything about it and change the world. The greater the change you want to make, the longer it will take. The larger the vision, the greater the effort it will take to achieve. The bigger the difference you want to make, the greater your commitment must be.

I think I should confess something to you, in light of the previous section. I have a bad habit of thinking that I am the exception to the rule. And it doesn't matter what the rule is. If there's a rule, my first thought is that I'm the exception to it. For example, I'll think, *I can still eat that double bacon cheeseburger with French fries and ranch dressing, but it won't affect my weight.* Or I'll think, *I don't need to train for that 10k; I'll just run a little bit next week be-fore the race.* Better still, *I can buy "that" now, even though I don't need it, and I'll still have plenty of money when I retire.* Even more, *I know every other first-time author has a hard time selling a thousand books, but I'll blow that out of the water.*

Now, I have no idea where this type of thinking comes from. The truth is, to change the world, to do something about it, you must realize something crucial: you will not be the exception to the rule. More importantly, you should not seek to be the excep-tion to the rule. I think it's obvious why we want to be the excep-tion—we believe it's easier, or rather, we *think* it's easier. As hu-mans, we drift towards the easier road.

Would you rather:

1. Win the lottery or work really hard for forty years?
2. Inherit a successful family business or start your own?
3. Use the fancy new ab machine for forty-three seconds three times a month, or eat healthy, cut back on sweets and soda, and work out six days a week to get a six-pack?
4. Lose fifty pounds by taking a little pill each day, or lose weight through diet and exercise?
5. Read the CliffsNotes, or read the whole book to get an A?

The path to doing something about it is not an easy one. If you are hoping your idea will be an overnight success, I need to warn you that you'll most likely be disappointed.

To Change the World, You Must Prepare

No one ever changed the world overnight.

No one ever went from last to first overnight.

Nothing great happens overnight... ever.

You may have some pushback on that, but give me a minute to explain. You see, most success stories are just that—stories. But they are usually the abridged version. Most of the time, we just read the headline and have no clue of the backstory. The headline reads, "New author sells million books" or "Rookie hits game-winning double in World Series." What the accurate headline should read for both of those stories is: "Guy who has been writing every day for the past ten years and who has repeatedly had every book proposal shot down in his face and told his writing stinks, kept on pursuing his dream and continued to write every day, and after all his hard work got a book deal and sold a lot of copies because he had lots of practice." Or "Baseball player who's been playing ball since age seven and played all the way through high school, then went to the minor leagues and traveled on a bus for half the year and got up every morning at 5:00 a.m. to work out and practice, got called up to the majors because fifteen years of working really hard with very little to show for it paid off as he got the winning hit in the World Series." But those are too long to serve as headlines! The point is, every success story has a long story behind it—not just a headline. Every success is set up by hard work beforehand. And if you want to be successful, preparation is the only way. If you want to change the world, you must prepare today.

Preparation is the first step to fully committing to doing something about it. This is true for all arenas of life. It's true in the sports world and in the business world. It's true in education and it's true in politics. It's true in marriage and it's true in the dating scene. More often than not, those who are most prepared are most successful. There are two different components of preparation: what you do and what God does. Let's look at God's part first.

◢   ◢   ◢

Just like Nehemiah, Moses, and John the Baptist, God is preparing you now for the things you will achieve later. This is true whether you realize it or not. God is always working, always planning, and always moving. Knowing this is what allows you to continue on your journey with a sense of peace. Without this truth, I—like most of you—would go crazy and never get anything accomplished. But how do we know God is working? How can we be sure? This is where our faith enters the equation. Many times, however, we will not realize the preparation until we're able to look back. In those moments of looking back, we often see the steps along the way that God used to get us where we currently are, and those memories help strengthen our faith for times of doubt in our future.

In the Old Testament, we find one of the best examples of God working behind the scenes to prepare a man to achieve his vision. Nehemiah was a man in an awkward position. When we first meet him, he was a Jewish exile who had become the cup-bearer for Artaxerxes, the king of Persia. This important detail to the story shows how God was preparing Nehemiah by enabling him to operate in proximity to those in power. Nehemiah discov-

ered that his own countrymen in Jerusalem were living in shame
because the walls to the city had been broken down. Jerusalem was
basically the laughingstock of the Middle East. As cupbearer, Nehemiah had direct connection with the king, and his job involved a
great amount of trust from the king. Nehemiah's main job was to
ensure that no one poisoned the king by slipping something in his
drink. This was definitely a job that the king checked references
on! After Nehemiah found out about the conditions in Jerusalem,
he was compelled to do something about it. Upon hearing the
news, Nehemiah sat down and wept. His spirit was literally broken
as he thought about Jerusalem. His next step is an important lesson for us—"*For some days I mourned and fasted and prayed before
the God of heaven*" (Nehemiah 1:4).

Once his burden became clear, Nehemiah mourned, fasted,
and prayed. Many of us, when we come face to face with a huge
problem, get so overwhelmed that we don't know what to do next.
If you find a problem that seems too big to even bother with, you
should follow Nehemiah's example—fast and pray.

I know the feeling all too well. When I helped start our ministry, World Causes, we wanted to help the 1.2 billion people who
live on $1 a day, but the problem seemed so big that we were fro-
zen with inactivity. As overwhelmed as he may have been, Nehemiah sat down and prayed. He got on his knees and asked God to
help him do something about what he had just heard. Nehemiah
recognized the role that only God could play and recognized the
exclusive position he was in as cupbearer to the king. Nehemiah
prayed,

> O Lord, let your ear be attentive to the prayer of
> this your servant and to the prayer of your ser-

vants who delight in revering your name. Give
your servant success today by granting him favor
in the presence of this man [the king]. (Nehemiah 1:11)

Prepare with Prayer

Prayer is the foundation of preparation. Prayer prepares your heart
to see and hear what God reveals to you. This lays the foundation
for your decisions. Prayer also allows your mind to take the right
perspective. Those who set out to accomplish anything without
prayer will fail before they reach the starting line. After thoroughly
praying for God's help, Nehemiah set out to take action, and when
he did we see how God's work behind the scenes was perfect in
enabling Nehemiah to achieve his vision. The next step for Nehemiah was to talk with the king and share his plan to rebuild the
walls. This is irony at its finest, because the rebuilt walls of Jerusalem would represent a direct threat to the king and his empire.
This is where we see that the prayers of Nehemiah were answered.

Nehemiah next determined what he needed to accomplish his
God-given vision and asked the king to provide what he needed to
rebuild the wall. He actually laid out a plan listing the physical re-
quirements that were necessary to rebuild a wall and the people he
needed to know to get it done.

If it pleases the king, may I have letters to the
governors of Trans-Euphrates, so that they will
provide me safe-conduct until I arrive in Judah?
And may I have a letter to Asaph, keeper of the
king's forest, so he will give me timber to make
beams for the gates of the citadel by the temple

and for the city wall and for the residence I will
occupy? (Nehemiah 2:7–8)

Nehemiah knew what he needed to accomplish his goal and
was prepared when the opportunity presented itself for him to act.
His preparation worked. *"And because the gracious hand of my God
was upon me, the king granted my requests"* (Nehemiah 2:8).

Your Move

We have a role to play when it comes to preparation. What are you
doing right now to prepare to accomplish your goals or ideas?
When I first felt the call to preach, I had absolutely no idea of
where that would take place or how. I didn't work at a church.
Most people who feel called to preach work at churches. Or, if
they don't have one they want to work at, they start one. Well, I fell
into neither one of those camps, but even so, the call to preach
remained. I wasn't going to start a church so I could preach. I had
been praying about it for years. I finally realized that I had to do
something beyond praying. I had to take the next step in preparation, which was essential for preaching. I had to start writing sermons. I came to realize that if God really was calling me to preach,
and someone actually wanted me to come preach, I had to have
something to say.

Now, I had plenty of stuff stored up in my mind, but that is
not the same thing as preparing. I needed to be prepared in a way
that would allow for effective communication. And if I was going
to be able to do this over the long haul, I needed good references.
Showing up unprepared is the easiest way to do a lousy job preaching, which in turns leads to fewer invitations. At first, as I began to

tell more people about this passion of mine to preach, I was overcome with the question of what I would do if I was asked to come
and speak on multiple occasions. If invitations did come, would I
be ready? Would I be prepared to act on this God-given idea? I
knew at that moment that the answer was *no*. So I began to study,
pray, and write sermons as if I was going to be giving one that very
week. Even though the opportunities were not yet coming on a
weekly basis, I knew that I had a part to play in the preparation,
just like God did. I took a seminary course on preaching. I began
spending time with other communicators, gleaning from them.

You see, I think our preparation is really a stewardship issue. If
God has called me to preach, did I really think he would give me
consistent places to preach if I wasn't prepared? Did I think I could
really preach to large crowds if I hadn't taken the time to plan for
it? If God has called you to do something, how you prepare reflects
the seriousness of your commitment to fulfill that call.

It's a Heart Issue

At the heart of preparation is stewardship. The importance we
place on preparation is equal to the importance we place on the
task at hand. You spend more time studying for a final exam than
you do for a weekly quiz. You spend more time (and energy and
focus) practicing for the state championship than you do for
spring practice. How we view the ultimate goal is revealed in our
preparation for that goal. Typical wisdom says that, if it's not that
important, don't waste time preparing for it; just wing it. If it's just
a quiz, cram in class the period before. If you're giving a presentation to a few people who have nothing to do with your future at
the company, there's no need to practice. If you are only leading

worship for thirty middle school students, there is no reason to put much effort in beforehand.

The problem with conventional wisdom is that it is often shot-blocked by Jesus. Jesus wasn't conventional and did not do what everyone else was doing. Jesus actually taught that the little things matter a lot. The stuff that no one thinks really "matters" is indeed very important. For in the small responsibilities, we see the heart of the individual. Jesus says that *"whoever can be trusted with very little can also be trusted with much, and whoever is dishonest with very little will also be dishonest with much"* (Luke 16:10).

I realized that my willingness to prepare sermons as if I was giving them to ten thousand people instead of thirty middle school students was a part of God testing me. If I thought I could wing it with thirty middle school students and God would still bless me to preach to ten thousand people, I was completely wrong. The same is true of you. If you think the small meetings don't matter, it shows what you can be trusted with. If you are not willing to work hard to lead the middle school kids in worship, God's not going to trust you with leading the two thousand students at your college either. Will you be a good steward of the opportunities God has given you? Will you view the thirty middle school kids not as something to get past so you can hunt larger prey but as an opportunity to serve God and prove yourself worthy of more?

I heard a pastor say it this way: God cares more about how you do it than where you do it and how much you make. In other words, God cares about the way you handle what he's given you right now. He's not as concerned about the next step as you are. He's not worried about the promotion or the increased salary, like you are. He's concerned with your effort now—he's concerned with your heart. He wants to see hard work now.

Paul taught this very thing in his letter to the Colossians. He tells them, *"Whatever you do, work at it with all your heart, as working for the Lord, not for men"* (Colossians 3:23). This means that if you are stacking chairs instead of leading worship, or working inventory instead of leading the company, do what God's given you right now with everything you have. What's interesting to note about this command from Paul is that he's writing to a group of Christian slaves. They wanted freedom more than you want to leave community college or get a promotion out of the mailroom. But Paul said that *"it is the Lord Christ you are serving"* (Colossians 3:24), so work with all your heart.

Moving On Up

As I mentioned earlier, in college I was leading worship for one of the largest campus ministries in the southeast. Toward the end of the first year, I started looking at who would take over for me when I graduated. I noticed Ronnie, a friend with loads of musical ability, but at the time he was not in the band. Actually, he was better at guitar than I was, had a better voice than me, and could play a couple other instruments. (Makes you wonder how I got the job in the first place, huh?) I knew that musical talent alone was not what made a good worship leader. The heart of the leader is what God is most concerned with. I also knew the principle that if my friend could be trusted with a little, he could be trusted with leading the ministry in worship.

The first task I asked of him was not to lead worship, nor was it to play guitar or even sing back-up. He wasn't even asked to play in the band. I asked him if he could help unload, set up, tear down, and reload our huge sound system each week. He accepted this with no complaints. After he did that for a few months, I asked him if he could help our sound engineer with the mixing, knowing he had a good musical ear. Well, for a few months this went on. Each Thursday he helped set up, tear down, and run sound. One week, we really needed a saxophone for a Dave Matthews song we were going to cover, and he happened to be an excellent saxophonist. He ended up playing sax for us for the rest of the semester and on into my senior year.

The first week of the spring semester of my senior year, I received a very unexpected phone call from Stevie, my friend and our lead guitarist. He'd decided to transfer to another school and would not be coming back. It was a sad time, as we'd been playing in the band together for a year and a half and had become like family. Well, we needed a new guitarist in a hurry. We had a worship service coming up in four days! At that point, it was a very simple decision about who would step in. Ronnie quit playing sax, took up lead guitar, and over the course of the semester he took over leading more songs until eventually he became the next worship leader. After graduation, he went on to lead worship at a church plant where he still leads today.

All of that is to say that the small stuff matters because it reveals the heart. Many times, we'll have no idea why we're unloading a truck instead of playing in the band. The truth is, playing in the band is a lot more fun than unloading a truck. But sometimes it's all a part of the journey. My friend's path to leading worship started with unloading speakers from a truck. My preaching started with preparing sermons for a crowd I hadn't even met yet. What do you need to start doing today in your process of doing something about it?

CHAPTER 7
TIMING AND PREPARATION

*"There are no secrets to success.
It is the result of preparation, hard
work, and learning from failure."*
—COLIN POWELL

It Took a Long Time to Create that Earth

One of the greatest literary works of the twentieth century was *The Lord of the Rings* trilogy by J.R.R. Tolkien. The books were eventually made into three movies, which together grossed just shy of $3 billion. The final installment, *Return of the King,* won eleven Oscars out of eleven nominations, including Best Picture. That is an extremely high honor and speaks well of everyone involved with making the film.

Tolkien began writing about Middle Earth, the fictional setting in which *Lord of the Rings* takes place, in 1937. In this make-believe world, Tolkien invented beautiful places filled with bizarre species with new languages. He wrote the backstory and history of his creation. Tolkien set out to tell a story but ended up creating a new world. When Tolkien finally finished writing the last of *The Lord of the Rings* trilogy, it was 1949. All in all, he worked over twelve years on his project of Middle Earth. Can you imagine working twelve years on a single project? To most people today, twelve years seems like an eternity to work at a job, much less write a book. But there's something powerful we can learn from Tolkien. He showed us that being dedicated to your vision and committing the time it takes to make it remarkable will pay off. Are you willing to commit a decade to seeing your dream reach its full potential?

One Year or Ten?

I have a confession to make. I am a goal setter. It's almost obsessive. I have one-year goals, three-year goals, ten-year goals, and life-long goals. I have goals for my spiritual growth. I set goals for my physical health. I have goals for how many books I want to read and how many blog posts and articles I want to write. I have goals for how many trips to take to the gym and how many pounds to lose. What I love about goals is that I always have something to shoot for. It's a self-imposed deadline that keeps me focused on what's important and motivates me in the downtimes. This past year, I set a goal to read fifty books. I was on track for most of the year.

"How many books have you finished?" my wife asked me. We were driving back from a family Thanksgiving gathering.

"I'm at forty-three."

"Ohh, you are so close to your goal. Do you think you can make it?" She's always encouraging me to accomplish my goals.

"We'll see. I'm in the middle of four books right now. If I can finish those, I still have to get through three more."

Three weeks later, I was three books away from my goal. We had driven down to see my wife's family in Florida for Christmas. I needed to find the time to fit in three more books. This proved to be difficult with all the meals together, playing board games, and ESPN showing a college football bowl game every night. I started sneaking away for a few hours at a time to squeeze in more reading time. I was staying up late trying to finish. I woke up on December 30 having just finished my forty-ninth book. I had one more to go.

"Did you do it?" my wife asked.

"One more to go," I said.

"You have two more days to do it," she said. "You can do it."

"I have to start a brand new one. I've finished all the ones I've started. Plus, we're driving all day tomorrow, so I have to finish it today," I said.

"Well, stay in the room until you do. You are so close to your goal!"

She was right. I was so close. I stayed up there all morning, and when I came down for lunch I was able to say that I had met my goal. And I had thirty-six hours to spare! I don't think I would have read so much had it not been for my goal. I know I wouldn't have focused so much that last week of the year had I not given myself the goal.

When it comes to fulfilling your passion or idea to change the world, you need to set for yourself realistic expectations of what you can accomplish and how long it will take you. Mark, a good friend and mentor of mine, says this, "We overestimate what we can accomplish in one year and underestimate what we can accomplish in ten."

I think he's right. When you first start pursuing your dream, if you overestimate what you will accomplish in the first year, you set yourself up for potential devastation if you don't meet your goals. The other side of that is the problem of underestimating what we can accomplish in ten years. When we do this, we sell ourselves—and our vision—short. We don't push as hard, because when we look around at our church plant of eighteen people or our non-profit with a $5,700 budget, we don't think we'll grow to 14,000 or $4,000,000 in the next ten years.

Mark told me his secret of avoiding falling into the overestimating and underestimating trap. He forces himself to think long, not big. Thinking long means committing to your idea (company, church, organization, causes, etc.) for a lengthy period and not allowing anything to derail that commitment. If you commit ten years to seeing your new idea get off the ground, gain traction, and ultimately accomplish what you want it to, you'll push right on through the dip period. The Dip, as author Seth Godin explains, is that time in the life cycle of an idea where it becomes really hard to keep going. It takes sacrifice, perseverance, and a genuine belief that it's worth pursuing to push through the Dip.

The reason so many have a hard time pushing through the Dip is that they have uncertainty in the vision or an unrealistic belief in their timeline. If you are uncertain of the vision, when it gets tough, finances get tight, or donations shrink you'll be more likely to quit. Similarly, if you have an unrealistic timeline—if you are not reaching your perceived goals in the first year or two—you'll also be tempted to quit. Thinking long overcomes these two main idea killers.

For many of you, you have a clear picture of what God is calling you to do. It may be preaching, youth ministry, or becoming a missionary. It may be teaching high school, starting a business, or even entering the political arena. There is nothing quite like feeling confident in a calling from God. Having clarity on where you are going with your career or ministry is awesome. It brings peace and confidence in decision-making. But what do we do when the call from God and opportunity to act seem further away than a white Christmas in Tahiti? What do we do when we have to wait?

The Waiting Game

John the Baptist had his future mapped out long before he could read or write. Before he visited any colleges or took any internships, God had a plan for John.

In Luke 1, let's start at the beginning of his story. Zechariah was a priest serving in the temple during the reign of Herod. He had a wife named Elizabeth and they had no children, *"because Elizabeth was barren; and they were both well along in years"* (Luke 1:7). If you think the odds are stacked against *you*, just look at this couple that's supposed to give birth to a world changer named John when both are old and the wife is barren. One day while Zechariah was serving in the temple, an angel of the Lord appeared to him and said:

> Do not be afraid, Zechariah; your prayer has
> been heard. Your wife Elizabeth will bear you a
> son, and you are to give him the name John. He
> will be a joy and delight to you, and many will re-
> joice because of his birth, for he will be great in
> the sight of the Lord. He is never to take wine or
> other fermented drink, and he will be filled with
> the Holy Spirit even from birth. Many of the
> people of Israel will he bring back to the Lord
> their God. And he will go on before the Lord, in
> the spirit and power of Elijah, to turn the hearts
> of the fathers to their children and the disobedi-
> ent to the wisdom of the righteous—to make
> ready a people prepared for the Lord. (Luke
> 1:13–17)

Wow! I bet Zechariah needed to change his pants. He had
been praying about having children for so long and now, when he
was old, he was finally going to get one. And here's the kicker—
this son was going to be the one who prepared the way for the
Lord! Zechariah wasn't just having any ordinary son; he was having a world changer. Zechariah told Elizabeth what happened, and
she was overwhelmed with joy. Nine months later, Elizabeth gave
birth to a son, and they named him John, just as the angel said they
should.

So the parents knew what John's path would look like. Now
the news spread to the neighbors.

> The neighbors were all filled with awe, and
> throughout the hill country of Judea people were
> talking about all these things. Everyone who
> heard this wondered about it, asking, "What then

is this child going to be?" For the Lord's hand
was with him. (Luke 1:65–66)

At this point, John was all of eight days old, and word was already spreading that he was called by God for a great task. Luke
said that even from birth, the Holy Spirit was upon John. So we
know that this was going to be a man passionate about his calling.
Once the neighbors were all talking about him, his dad was filled
with the Holy Spirit and prophesied about him:

> And you, my child, will be called a prophet of the
> Most High; for you will go on before the Lord to
> prepare the way for him, to give his people the
> knowledge of salvation through the forgiveness
> of their sins, because of the tender mercy of our
> God, by which the rising sun will come to us
> from heaven to shine on those living in darkness
> and in the shadow of death, to guide our feet into
> the path of peace. (Luke 1:76–79)

John's calling was clear. His purpose was to prepare the way
for Jesus' message and ministry. I don't think he had much of a
choice in the matter, either. I mean, think about what his childhood must have been like. His parents kept reminding him, as he
was studying, that he was going to do great things. His neighbors
whispered about him as he walked by. Friends at school did the
same thing. He might have been ridiculed by some; we don't
know. But there is no doubt that he was reminded all the time
about what his calling was.

The last verse in Luke 1 reveals something about John's journey at a point when he probably got bogged down. *"And the child*

grew and became strong in spirit; and he lived in the desert until he appeared publicly to Israel" (Luke 1:80). There are a few points to consider in this verse. First, John grew. This is probably referring to more than just height and weight. John knew from a young age what he was called to do and that it would take lots of preparation. If he was to call an entire nation back to God, it would require a lot of skill and a very deep relationship with God. Second, he became strong in spirit. This is the spiritual growth component. This probably included spending time in prayer, studying the scriptures, fasting, meditating, and preparing his message. Third, he went and lived in the desert until he appeared publicly. Can you imagine how hard this must have been for him? He knew what his calling was. He knew what his role would be. He had a growing passion to prepare the way for the Lord, yet he was out living in the desert. Odds are he had a view of Jerusalem from where he lived. He could probably see it in the distance. No doubt, he saw people coming and going from the city on a daily basis. He was staring at his calling for years before he was able to act on it. Seeing the lights of the city at night and hearing the crowds during the day must have been agonizing for him. He'd heard all his life that he would be preaching there some day to prepare the way of the Lord.

The waiting must have been the lowest point in his life. Or maybe it wasn't. Maybe John had such peace with his calling that he focused his time and energy on being prepared for his time instead of just sitting around and waiting for it to arrive. Maybe he practiced baptizing people or calling out Pharisees. We don't know what he was doing, but what we do know is that when his time came, he was well-prepared for his ministry. Luke tells us in the third chapter of his gospel that people from all over began to come out to see John after the word of the God came to him in the desert. He went all around the countryside preaching a baptism of repentance for the forgiveness of sins. Crowds came from miles around, including tax collectors and soldiers, to hear what John had to say. But none of that would have been possible if John had not been prepared. Had he not spent days, months, and years preparing for his ministry, it would not have been successful.

The same is true of anyone who has ever done anything great in the world. They were prepared for the time when they would make their impact. It was the same for John the Baptist as it is today for you. If you want to do something to change the world, you have to prepare first and then trust God's timing. John knew his calling and spent the necessary time preparing for his ministry, so once called he was able to fulfill his calling with excellence. Maybe you are sitting there feeling a calling on your life to do something great, but it seems that all you are doing is waiting. How does one wait well?

What is it you want to do? Do you want to be a teacher, a lawyer, or professional skateboarder? Do you want to preach, lead worship, or be a missionary? Maybe you dream of starting a business, being an author, or running for office. Whatever it is you feel called to do, you will never be successful unless you start preparing today.

Are you reading the right books?

Are you meeting with people who have done what you want to do?

Are you taking classes or workshops?

Are you going on trips with your church?

Are you reading the Word?

Are you practicing in the half-pipe?

Are you spending time writing every day?

If you are not taking action now, you will not be prepared when opportunity knocks. One of the lessons I've learned is that the more I prepare, the more opportunities God seems to send my way. You need to view your preparation as an opportunity from God—it is literally a gift. It is not something to be spurned, but rather embraced.

White House or Bust

It is said that Abraham Lincoln felt called to greatness as a young man. Growing up on different farms in Kentucky, Indiana, and Illinois, Lincoln fought uphill all the way to become President of the United States. His mother died when he was nine and his father was an illiterate, uneducated carpenter and hired hand. Between working for the family and on the farm, Lincoln said that if you were to add his entire time in school, *it would not even add up to an entire year*. He admitted later in life that all of his education was self-taught. It is said that he would read any book he could get his hands on. And in a day without Barnes and Noble or Amazon.com, he would sometimes travel great distances to get his hands on a new book. Listen to how he prepared while in the waiting process:

> Everywhere he went, Lincoln carried a book with him. He thumbed through page after page while his horse rested at the end of a long row of planting. Whenever he could escape work, he would lie with his head against a tree and read... with remarkable energy and tenacity he quarried the thoughts and ideas that he wanted to remember.[5]

Lincoln was so determined to achieve his passion that he would not let his current circumstances slow his progress. This progress came at a social cost, too, but Lincoln was willing to climb over that wall to reach his goal. He was considered awkward in public, but that didn't stop him. It was something to get past to achieve his goal. He didn't waste time; he was usually working or reading.

In the pioneer world of rural Kentucky and Indiana, where physical labor was essential for survival and mental exertion was rarely considered a legitimate form of work, Lincoln's book hunger was regarded as odd and indolent. Nor would his community understand the thoughts and emotions stirred by his reading; there were few to talk to about the most important and deeply experienced activities of his mind.[6]

Maybe you can connect with Lincoln's situation. Maybe the people in your life, like your parents or siblings, don't understand why you go to church or want to read your Bible. Maybe everyone in the family is a lawyer who doesn't get why you want to be a teacher. Just like Lincoln, you will have to get over the wall of caring what people think to reach your goal and ultimately change the world.

The story of Abraham Lincoln fascinates me as I consider my own journey. I look at the resources available to me, my education, my personal library, the Internet, my mentors who have volumes of experience and wisdom, and I contrast it all with what Lincoln had. There is no comparison. I've come to find out that it doesn't matter what resources you have if you do not use them. The same is true of information and learning. It doesn't matter what you know; it matters what you do with what you know. Lincoln went on to teach himself law, passed the state bar exam, practiced law before he entered politics, and ultimately achieved the highest office in the nation.

So what are you doing while you are waiting? How are you spending your time? Are you looking at all the odds stacked against you, or are you doing everything you can to turn the tables? How are you growing? Remember to think long.

1O,OOO Hours

In *Outliers,* Malcolm Gladwell's remarkable book on the topic of success, he looks at the lives of the extremely successful to find out what truly made them a success. He looked at people like billionaire Bill Gates and the Beatles. He looked at the best hockey players from Canada and the most sought-after lawyers in New York. What is interesting about his findings is that, aside from lucky breaks and once-in-a-lifetime opportunities, the most obvious characteristic of the truly successful is the amount of practice they put into their given field. With Gates, it was the number of hours he spent computer programming. With the Beatles, it was the number of live performances they staged. What separates the good from the best is that the best put in 10,000 hours of practice. That's 10,000 hours of computer programming, 10,000 hours of live performances, and 10,000 hours of practicing law. Without exception, the best worked harder than those who are merely good and put in 10,000 hours to make it there.

However you are trying to change the world, you need to know that the greater the change you want to make, the longer it will take to succeed. But if you know this going in and are willing to commit for the long run and work hard, there is no doubt you will change the world. Think long, not big. Take time to prepare.

Define Success

One of the first things you need to come to terms with is deter-
mining what success looks like for you and your new venture. If
you were given unlimited resources, what would success look like?
If you had zero resources, what would success look like? If your
goal is to rescue victims of injustice, how many will you have to
save to be successful? One? One million? If your goal is to start a
business, how much profit equals success? If your goal is to write a
book, how many books do you have to sell for it to be a success?

When I was trying to define success for this book, I decided
that one life greatly impacted would be enough. That means if I
sell one book to get that or a million, success is not found in the
number of books sold, but in the outcomes of the readers' lives.
Now, I know that sounds super cheesy, but one of the great lessons I have learned is that the influence of one person can change
history. All it takes is one person to say yes and to accept the call to
change the world. All it takes is one person to commit twenty years
to abolishing the slave trade to change history. Nelson Mandela,
Martin Luther King Jr., William Wilberforce, Billy Graham... it
only takes one to respond. That person could be you. That's why
success for this book is having one life greatly impacted—thus
responding and changing the world.

Defining success will help sustain you through the dark days
and the cold nights. This is another lesson in thinking long, not
big. When you define success, you have a holistic perspective of
current circumstances. If you plant a church and only three people
show up (counting you, your wife, and your son), but success is

seeing life change in your city, you will keep meeting until you see it.

This happened to a friend of mine. The first week of his church launch, no one came. It was just him and his family. While it was hard to swallow that morning, he was able to keep pushing because success was not defined by how many people showed up the first week. Success was defined by seeing people's lives changed. Now, thousands of lives have been changed, and the church is almost fifteen years old. Don't confuse success with short-term results. Ninety-nine percent of you are running a marathon, so the first few days, months, or even years are just a fraction of the whole vision. Don't get bogged down or depressed in the very beginning. Keep pushing towards your complete definition of success, even if it takes twenty years.

CHAPTER 8
A DIFFERENT PATH

"It's not that I'm so smart,
it's just that I stay with
problems longer."
—ALBERT EINSTEIN

That's Not What I Signed Up For!

Without thinking, Vince asked, "What's for dinner?" He knew the answer. It was the same answer he got every other night that month: peanut butter and jelly sandwiches. It was all he could afford, and he wasn't sure for how much longer, either.

"Vince, there's a notice from the bank," his wife said.

It had been weeks since their last paycheck. They were now behind on the mortgage and late on the power bill. They had to drop the insurance, and now there was another notice from the bank.

It was a long drive home for Vince. He was seriously considering walking away this time. He'd entertained the thought numerous times over the previous few years, but none as serious as this. It had now been over two months since his last paycheck and he was sick of peanut butter.

When he got home, he sat down and started crying out to God. "What would you have me do?" he asked. He was reminded of the prayer he prayed just before his twenty-first birthday, when he surrendered his life to Christ. "God, if this is real, all I want to do is make a difference. I don't want to go through the motions of life. I want to make a difference for you. It doesn't matter where; just use me." He was the one who asked God to use him. He started to realize he was getting that prayer answered.

Vince believed God had given him a vision to change the inner city of Atlanta. He knew in his heart that he was being obedient to that vision. That next morning, he kept thinking, "What if I walk away today, and then God opens the floodgates and fulfills the vision tomorrow? I don't think I could live with that. I will regret it every day for the rest of my life." He knew he had to keep going. He wasn't sure how, but Vince knew quitting was not an option.

Three weeks later, Vince was in Florida for some meetings when a good friend called to invite him over for lunch. He was a long-time supporter of Vince's ministry and had no idea of the financial situation Vince was in. After a nice lunch, his friend said,

"Let's take a walk around the lake. I want to hear how things are going."

"I'm pretty sure he doesn't," was all Vince could think.

"So, how are things with you and the family?" he asked.

"The new ministry with the schools is going amazing," Vince responded.

"Great. But how are things with you and your family?" he repeated.

It had now been thirteen weeks without a paycheck, and late notices had flooded Vince's mailbox.

"We're expecting to reach more kids this year than any other year since we've been in ministry. We've very excited." All of this was true about the ministry, but Vince knew he was avoiding the actual question.

The friend stopped walking and turned and looked Vince in the eye and said, "That's fine. But I want to know how you and your family are doing."

Vince looked into his eyes and could not hide it any longer. Tears began to flow, and he broke down. A floodgate of emotions came pouring out.

"Things aren't good," he sobbed. "We're about to lose everything. Not only personally, but also in the ministry. We have notices for the mortgage, cars, and all the utilities. I don't understand why it's all happened. I haven't taken a paycheck in thirteen weeks. We had to drop the insurance, and I would be fine never seeing another peanut butter and jelly sandwich."

They both had a little laugh about the peanut butter comment.

"And I can look you in the eye and tell you we've done nothing illegal or immoral in the ministry," Vince continued. "We've been obedient to the call God's given us. We just don't have any money." Vince was so tired, but it felt so good to get this out. Now, at least someone else knew.

His friend looked at him with tears in his eyes and said, "Denise and I have always believed in you guys."

He was right. They were great friends and had been some of his most faithful supporters.

"So, consider all your bills paid in full. How much do you need?"

Vince could not believe it. He started crying even more. Between tears, he listed everything they needed, the total came to more than $20,000.

"When do you need it by?" he asked.

He glanced down at his watch. It was ten minutes after noon.

"Ten minutes ago," Vince said. The bank had given them until noon to catch up or they were going to start repossessing everything they owned.

"Get on the phone with your wife. Tell her to call the bank and the creditors. They'll all be paid in full by Monday next week."

Early the next week, Vince received a call to let him know that all the transfers had been made.

"I'm not sure exactly why, but the Lord impressed on me to include an extra $5,000. Hopefully, that can give you a little cushion through this next season," his friend said.

When they got off the phone, Vince and his wife sat down to make sure everything was squared away. As it turned out, they had forgotten to include the difference from the last billing cycle until the time the talk around the lake took place. They actually owed $4,900 more dollars. After everything was paid off, there was $100 left in their account.

Vince's story has always been an inspiration to me. After listening to him recall the past fifteen years of his life, I asked him, "Was it worth it?"

"Was it worth it?" he echoed. "Absolutely. Without a doubt, it was worth it. It was hard. It challenged my faith in ways I never would have imagined. But looking back, I wouldn't change a thing. Our two sons and daughter now want to be in full-time ministry when they graduate college. We've seen 10,000 kids hear the gospel through our ministry. There have been 17,000 short-term missionaries come though us to be educated and given opportunities to serve inner cities. Even though we don't have 401Ks or know how we're paying for our children's college, it was worth it!"

I asked one final question. "How did you stay committed through all of that?"

"I knew it wouldn't be easy. Staying grounded in our faith gave us the strength to stick with it. If we wouldn't have believed that God called us and that he was able to meet our needs, we would have quit a long time ago. I'm thankful we didn't."

Where's My Burning Bush?

What do you do when your idea takes a different path than the one you planned? What happens when the timetable is nowhere close to what you thought? What would you do if your idea took forty years longer than expected? Moses' path to changing the world took a different and much longer road than he hoped.

Moses had it made. He was a child of privilege, raised in the palace by Pharaoh's daughter. Anything he needed was available to him. But Moses was the exception to the rule. He was a Hebrew living in the Egyptian palace. His fellow countrymen were slaves working for Pharaoh. Moses had no idea what life was like for the typical Hebrew. One day, this all changed.

When Moses was older, he went out to where his fellow Israelites "worked," and what he saw disturbed him. He did not see workers. He saw slaves. Maybe he felt the guilt of living in luxury by the slave labor of his own people. Whatever he thought, when he saw the injustice, he wanted to stop it, so he acted on impulse. As he got closer, he saw a Jew being beaten. Looking over his shoulder to ensure no one was watching, Moses killed the Egyptian slave driver and buried the body in the sand. When word of the attack spread back to Pharaoh, Pharaoh tried to kill Moses, so he hit the road to save his life. Forty years later, we find Moses on the backside of a mountain.

For forty years, Moses has been carrying the guilt of his action and the passion of the injustice he saw in the slave fields. This is the precise moment that God walked by and showed up in a burning bush. Moses was intrigued by a flaming bush that was not burning. He took a closer look. Just like with James and John, God showed up at a time when his call would force Moses to decide to change the world or stay with the family business.

Moses was the head shepherd for Jethro, his father-in-law. He had it cozy once again. He knew where his income would come from. He knew where he would live. He knew he would be at peace with his family. Well, that is, until God showed up. And just like Moses, you'll know when God walks by. The call is unmistakable. CONTINUE FROM HERE

> The Lord said, "I have indeed seen the misery of my people in Egypt.[7] I have heard them crying out because of their slave drivers, and I am con-

cerned about their suffering. So I have come
down to rescue them from the hand of the Egyptians and to bring them up out of that land into a
good and spacious land, a land flowing with milk
and honey—the home of the Canaanites, Hit-
tites, Amorites, Perizzites, Hivites and Jebusites.
And now the cry of the Israelites has reached me,
and I have seen the way the Egyptians are op-
pressing them. So now, go. I am sending you to
Pharaoh to bring my people the Israelites out of
Egypt." (Exodus 3:7–10)

Moses was getting a little excited at this point. I mean, this was
exactly how he had felt when he saw the slavery, and it was why he
had decided to kill one of the slave drivers. Moses wanted justice.
His passion was still alive, but as we all do, he had doubts. I mean,
his passion was forty years old. Now he was a family man. He had
responsibilities. He had mouths to feed. He had a job. His father-
in-law needed him for the business. Plus, he was a shepherd. We
can imagine him saying, "I lead sheep, not people. I don't know
how you free a nation. I mean, what if no one believes me? What if
they say no? And how in the world am I to prove to them that you
sent me?"

We're not sure what more Moses wanted to do the day he
killed the Egyptian slave driver. We don't know if he wanted to
raise an army or start a rebellion. We know he wanted justice, but
that's all. When God finally intervened on Moses' behalf, he sent
Moses right back where he didn't want to go. Moses didn't want to
face Pharaoh. Pharaoh had tried to kill him years ago. This was not
the path of choice for Moses. Certainly there had to be another
way. Still, Moses wanted to stop the injustice the Hebrews were

suffering at the hands of the Egyptians. God just took a little longer to answer than Moses wanted. And God chose a different path than Moses expected!

Sometimes God calls us to fulfill a burden years after it is born. For Moses, it was forty years later. Many people give up in the waiting period because it takes too long. Many people quit because they don't recognize that the way God is leading them down is the path. Moses is a great example that even when it takes a long time, God is faithful to fulfill the desires he has given you, especially the ones that involve changing the world.

In his letter to the Galatians, Paul writes a great word of encouragement for times when it seems God is taking too long: *"Let us not become weary in doing good, for at the proper time we will reap a harvest if we do not give up"* (Galatians 6:9).

Needs to Control Talking

A few years ago, when I was packing up a bunch of stuff from my mom's house, I ran across my old report cards from elementary school. It was slightly embarrassing to read some of the remarks that were made about me. Now, I was mostly an A, and sometimes B, student. I didn't fail any grades or anything like that. What I'm referring to is my conduct. I got "Needs to control conduct" checked on my six-week progress reports more often than not. In fact, I got "Needs to control talking" checked every six weeks from kindergarten through fifth grade!

At the time, that was not funny. I can remember being grounded because I talked too much. But what my teachers saw as a kid who talked too much, God saw as a future preacher of the gospel. You see, God knows how it all comes together. I do not believe there are any accidents in God's economy. He is always working. He is always preparing. What seems like a dead-end to you may actually be the preparation you need for God to use you to change the world.

When I question why something is happening the way it is, I remind myself that God is still working, he is still planning, and he will still use me, even if it's in a way I don't know about yet. I don't think Moses thought he was getting anywhere closer to stopping the injustice of the Hebrew slaves when he was tending sheep, but the skills he learned there prepared him like no one else to lead the Israelites out of Egypt and into the Promised Land. Moses spent the next forty years shepherding a million people instead of sheep.

Picture Perfect

A good friend of mine is a local photographer. He loves his job and is really talented. That is a good combination. One day, he started telling me about this event he was putting together with some local photographers to serve some of the city's homeless and unfortunate families. A few weeks before Christmas, they were going to give away free professional portraits to individuals and families. Anyone was welcome. At the end of the day, Jeff said that many people came, and almost all were overwhelmed by the generosity of the event. A handful of photographers made a huge impact. One man in his late forties said that was the first time anyone had ever taken his picture. It was a day to remember.

I found out some amazing details a few weeks later. It turns out that Jeff and his crew were one of about 4500 groups setting up events like that all around the world that day to serve their cities. Later I found something even more amazing. This event was titled Help Portrait and was started by Jeremy just four months before. In four months, Help Portrait went from an idea in Jeremy's head to 4500 events around the world.

I was able to catch up with him and learn more about how it happened.

"I've only been a professional photographer for about four years," he told me. In that short four-year stretch, he's worked with the likes of Fox Network and dozens of bands, was the tour photographer for one of Britney Spears' tours, and has become the photographer of choice for many bands, authors, and actors.

"I wanted to use photography to do something to give back," he continued. "I'd been talking with some other photographers, and we decided to do a little event in Nashville. Eight of us got together and took portraits of the homeless and gave them free prints. In all, we only served about sixty people, but it was a great event. We posted some stories online to share what had happened and we had no idea what would happen afterward. I posted a short video of the event and the idea started spreading to other photographers. We posted the video in August, and on December 7 of that year we had 40,000 portraits taken in 42 countries in the first annual Help Portrait. CNN and CBS Evening News covered the story, and it just began to blow up."

Jeremy's story is a great example of how being used by God to change the world may look nothing like you thought it would. Here was a guy who wanted to be a painter growing up and wound up in graphic design. From there, he went on to become a brilliant photographer, and then God allowed him to leverage that gift to serve 40,000 people. Note, this is not a full-time job for Jeremy. As of now, Help Portrait happens only one day a year.

CHAPTER 9
OVERCOMING OBSTACLES

*"If you can find a path with
no obstacles, it probably
doesn't lead anywhere."*
—FRANK A. CLARK

Obstacles to Doing Something About It

After finding your calling, obstacles will immediately surface and attempt to snuff out the fire of your passion. The responsibilities of life will scream like a megaphone in your ear. Many times, the person holding the megaphone is someone very close to you who loves you and wants the best for you. It may be a spouse, parent, or best friend. One or more of these people will give their advice and it may *seem* very logical, but keep this

one thing in mind: they aren't called to do something about *it*—
you are! To be faithful to that calling, you have to care more about
what God thinks than what they think.

Africa's Not for You

When my wife was in college, she really felt called to go to the nation of Ethiopia in Africa.

"It's not like I want to go forever," she said one day. "I just feel
like I should go."

"So, how did it go when you talked with your parents?" I
asked. Seeing the expression on her face, I could figure out it
wasn't good.

"I told them I wanted to go over the summer. It would just be
for a couple of months."

I knew she'd been praying about it most of the semester. She
was so excited when we talked about it. We were certain her parents would support the idea. They'd always supported her in other
areas of her life.

"Well, what did they say?"

"They didn't say much at first," she told me. "Which was not a
good sign. I could tell instantly that they were not excited. After a
few minutes, they listed a bunch of reasons why I shouldn't go—
You're too young. You'll be by yourself. You won't know anyone
over there. It's too dangerous. It was all a bunch of generic stuff." I
could tell she was upset.

"They just don't get it, I guess," she said. "In the end, they said
they didn't want me going."

She was crushed. Was there a good reason for their answer?
Not really. They didn't feel the call that Betsey had and couldn't

understand why she would want to go. She was upset. She prayed. She sought advice. Ultimately, the summer came and went and she never made it to Africa. But she had decided that pleasing God was more important than any idea she had, so she respected her parents' decision and stayed home.

Fast forward seven years, and we have started a ministry to help those suffering from poverty, including some places in Africa. If you are experiencing something similar to this story, you may question the call or burden from God. You must remember that God's call and his timing are two different issues.

Leaving the Family Business

There are two brothers I want to thank when I get to heaven—and you should, too—for their willingness to care more about pleasing God than anyone else. You see, at the moment of their decision, they probably had no idea of the eternal significance that hung in the balance. And many times, neither will you.

These two brothers were set to take over their father's business. They had learned the business in and out. They had prepared. They were ready… until Jesus came walking by. James and John, the sons of Zebedee in Galilee, were fishermen, and probably pretty good ones at that. As their father looked over his business plan, it most likely involved handing the business over to his sons. It was his plan to retire with some sort of security. Dad had a lot of his future riding on his sons.

For James and John, it was a pretty good deal. Their dad had built the business. He most likely had a good customer base, a good marketing plan, a Twitter account, Facebook fanpage, and a very up-to-date website. The infrastructure was in place, including all the equipment, boats, and nets he needed for a successful fishing business. To all those looking in, it made perfect since for James and John to be fishermen. It made perfect since—that is, for everyone except three people: James, John, and Jesus.

I cannot prove this, but I have an idea that neither James nor John knew what they would do if they did not take over the family business. I think there was a desire in them for something greater, something beyond fishing, but I don't know if they could put their fingers on it. I don't think they had a clue that they would go on to be the founders of the Christian Church and write letters that would be part of the new Scriptures that would change the face of the planet like no other movement in the history of the world. The truth is, neither will you know the magnitude of how your decision will affect the world.

James and John literally changed the world by taking the first step of choosing to please God over their father. I mean, think about this for a moment. What if they had stayed in the boats? What would the church look like today without them? What if they would have said, "You know, Jesus, following you might be fun, but we're not really sure where we'll live or what we'll eat. We don't know how we will provide for our families. We're not really trained to change the world. I think we'll stick with the plan that makes the most logical sense and has the lowest amount of risk involved. I mean, that's what people expect from us. Our dad was a fisherman, so was granddad, and his dad before him. We have our degrees in fishing. We have a lot of money invested in this business. And what about our dad? He's depending on us to take it over for him so he can have a decent retirement. Jesus, thanks for the invite to change the world, but I think we're going to stick it out here and see what happens."

It's hard to image that conversation because we know the end of the story. We know they chose to follow Jesus instead of staying. We know they went on to follow Jesus, build his church, and write parts of the New Testament. We know they changed the world. We know that because we can see the end of the story, but they couldn't see their end, and neither will you see yours.

Now, this is not a free pass to ignore good opportunities like taking over a family business or following in the footsteps of your mother or father. The point is *not* to avoid being like your parents. The point is wanting to please God more than anyone else, including your parents. And when you do this, you will ultimately have to make decisions they might not agree with or support. When that happens, will you choose to change the world, or will you choose the path of least resistance?

The awesome part of this story is that James and John didn't just leave their boats for some harebrained idea. They just responded to Jesus when he called them. I believe that along the way, they felt a stirring inside them to something beyond fish guts and late nights. There were probably times when they were pulling in nets when they questioned, "Why are we doing this?" These little promptings and questions brought them to the point where when Jesus called, they were able to drop their nets and walk away.

Spring Break-Up

When I was in high school, my dad had a dream for me: that I would be a golf superstar. He taught me how to play when I was six. I played in my first tournament at the age of nine and got second place. He was so proud. I continued playing in tournaments through middle school and high school. I liked golf, but I don't think I liked it quite as much as he did. My love was for basketball. I lived and breathed basketball. That is, until sophomore year, when I was the last person cut from the junior varsity team. I thought I had made the team. I had made it through tryouts, and we were in the second week of practice. There were only nine of us on the team, and I got called into the coach's office after practice and he told me it was my last practice. My heart broke. I didn't understand. I was ticked off, too. (This is where it would be awesome to tell my own Michael Jordan story about how I came back and made the team and broke records and yada yada yada. But my story doesn't end that way. It ends better!)

While all my friends were headed to Florida for spring break, I was practicing for a golf tournament qualifier that would take place that weekend. I remember thinking, *Is this what I want? Wouldn't I rather be in Florida with all my friends?* The answer was no, this was not what I wanted. So when I ended up not qualifying for the event, I decided to drive down to Florida to stay with some friends. It ended up being the beginning of the end. When I got home, I was working through the internal struggle of what to do with my golf future. I didn't think that was where I wanted to be, but all the outside circumstances seemed right. My dad had invested a lot in me. I had the talent, if I would only put in the time and sacrifice.

Then I had my very own James and John moment where Jesus walked by. I had gotten more involved with my youth group that year. I was spending a lot of time with one of our leaders, and he was an amazing worship leader. The thought of leading worship began to pop in my mind. But I didn't know how to play guitar, I hadn't been formally trained to sing, and by the way, I didn't even

own a guitar. That all began to change one day when a friend came
over for a visit.

"What are you doing today?" I asked Joey over the phone.

"Not much," he said.

"Why don't you come over in a few minutes? I've got a crazy
idea."

When Joey got to my house, we climbed into my white 1987
Honda Civic with no air conditioning and headed to the interstate.
It was a beautiful spring day. The windows were down and the CD
was playing. This would be a day to remember.

"You want to tell me where we're going now?" Joey asked.

"Yeah. I've got to go shopping."

"What?!? You wanted me to come over to go shopping with
you?"

"Oh, trust me. You'll like where we're going," I said confidently. Joey had started playing guitar recently, so he'd love to
hang out in a guitar superstore for a few hours.

We headed down the interstate, and as I pulled off the exit,
there was the huge sign. I could see Joey's face get excited. As we
pulled in, he asked, "So, we're going shopping here?"

"Yeah, I think I'm going to buy a guitar today. A nice one,
too," I said.

We walked into the store and there were guitars everywhere.
There was a giant wall of electric guitars on the left. We walked
through the drums and amplifiers to the back where there was a
special room for acoustic guitars. There were hundreds of options.

"Dang! Look at all these guitars," I said. "I have no idea what
to get."

The walls of the room were lined with guitars. Joey started
picking up different ones and playing the songs he knew. I decided

to do the same. As I was looking over all the names and brands, I picked up a shiny Takamini G Series acoustic/electric guitar. It was beautiful.

"I'll take it!" I said. "This is the one, Joey."

I showed it to him, and he loved it, too. I headed to the checkout counter. As we walked out the door, I had no idea how much that decision would change my life.

So I haven't mentioned where I got the money to buy the guitar. There just happened to be enough money in my account for a few golf tournaments that were scheduled for later in the year. I decided a guitar was the better investment. The hard part was going to be breaking the news to my dad. I wanted my dad to be proud of me. I knew he wanted me to be a golfer. He had big plans. Dropping the nets is not easy. One reason is that it affects more than just yourself.

It wasn't just me who was affected by my decision to leave competitive golf and pursue music. My dad would be drastically affected. At this point, I had to face the music—actually, my dad had to face my music! I had to tell my dad that, even though I had no previous music experience, I was quitting golf to pursue playing the guitar. Even though I had been playing competitive golf for more than a decade, it was over for me, and it was over for him.

Now, we don't know how James' and John's dad reacted when they said they were going to follow Jesus. Did he yell, "You're crazy!" or did he hug them and encourage them along the way? We don't know. I was nervous to tell my dad the decision to quit competitive golf. Would I let him down? Would he be mad? Would he want the money back? Would I have to sell my brand new guitar and give back the money? These were all the thoughts running through my head. I knew that my dad could sense that something had changed in me.

When I finally told him what I'd done, I knew he was disappointed, but he chose to support my decision anyway. It was a real turning point in my relationship with him. No one wants to let down his father, including me. I imagine he was thinking this would just be a fluke and that I was wasting an opportunity to excel in golf. A few years later, when I was leading worship for one of the largest campus ministries in the nation, my dad actually bought me a new and much nicer guitar. It was an amazing moment for me in my faith as I recognized that God was in control and that he blesses us when we are obedient to him.

When I dropped the nets of golf, like James and John dropped their nets, it actually gave my dad an opportunity to drop his nets of me becoming a star golfer, and because of that our relationship was better than ever. Plus, playing golf with my dad now is one of my favorite things to do in the world. It all turned out well in the end, but going through the process was not easy, because the fear of disappointing your family can be devastating.

Decision Time

Looking back, I had no idea what hung in the balance of that decision. Here is a quick map of the events that took place because I threw down my nets and took a trip to Guitar Center. I helped lead worship during my senior year of high school at church. I went on to college and led worship at various high school Fellowship of Christian Athletes (FCA) groups. I then led worship for an entire summer of mission trips (which is where I heard the call to preach). I then went on to lead worship services for the largest college FCA in the nation. I spent a summer in Africa and got to lead worship there. I went on to help start a college ministry at a church in Texas after I graduated college. I mentored one worship leader who is now a worship leader at a growing church, and through all those experiences the call to preach was cultivated, which is now where God is leading me full-time.

These are just the things I know about. You can never know the impact you've made on everyone who has ever been in your ministry. With thousands of students each year coming to our services, I don't have a clue what impact I made on most of them. But one thing I do know—there is no way I would have done anything mentioned above without my dropping the nets of golf and going to Guitar Center. There are eternal consequences that hang in the balance of your decisions that you may never know about. James and John didn't have any idea what hung in the balance of their decision to drop their nets and follow Jesus.

Are there nets in your life that you need to drop? Maybe it's your college decision, your career path, or the family business. Maybe it's a dating relationship that is leading you where you don't want to go. If you want to change the world, you will have to throw down your nets and pursue your passion and ideas. By doing this, you show yourself and the world that you care more about pleasing God than anyone else. Decide today that you will seek to please God over everyone else. By doing so, you will change the world in greater ways than you ever thought possible.

Now, there's just one more person to convince that you can change the world.

Get Out of Your Own Way

When it comes to pursuing that dream you have, one of the hardest people to convince that you can actually do it is the person you look at in the mirror each morning. That's right, it's you. Many times others believe in us more than we believe in ourselves. We are our own worst enemies. How many dreams, businesses, churches, ministries, books, or paintings were killed before they had a chance to get off the ground because the person talked themselves out of starting it? My bet would be a huge number. You don't want to add to it.

Once you've decided to do something about it, you need to know that you'll still be tempted along the way to give up, to quit, to shut it down. You'll wake up one morning and question everything: *Why did I start this church? Why am I trying to accomplish something so big? Why did I quit my job for this? Why did I move here? Why? Why? Why?* I still have these moments. And I think any person who changed the world would share the same story. Just because you sign up doesn't mean you'll never question again.

So, you need to get out of your own way. I know this is easier said than done, but this is a requirement in order to do something about it. Getting out of your way requires you to ask good questions. Good questions help you change the world, but bad questions will stop you dead in your tracks.

Most of the time, bad questions are good questions asked at the wrong time. Let's say you find your *it* and decide to do something about *it*. You decide the best step is to start a local nonprofit. Here are a few good questions you should ask:

Why am I doing this?

Is starting this what God has for me?

Do I have a plan to make this happen?

Is this worth the risk?

Why don't I have the support of my closest friends and family?

Am I willing to work overtime to see this venture succeed?

These are good questions to ask in the beginning, because they help you establish your goal and solidify your purpose. If you don't set a goal or purpose you are aiming for, you'll subconsciously set one that could take you off your intended path.

After you ask these questions, the next step is to get honest answers. This is crucial. If you can honestly and confidently answer the good questions in the beginning, you are well on your way to getting out of your way!

Now, the next phase is when you are well into your journey, and you'll know you're there because you'll hit some type of wall. Walls come in all shapes and sizes and may look like any of these:

You run out of money.

You get a rejection letter from a key donor.

Volunteers leave.

No one comes to the fundraiser.

You're not growing as fast as planned.

At this point, the future of *it* rests in the questions you ask next. If you ask good questions, you'll be able to get out of your own way and persevere until you get the results you intended in the beginning. If you ask bad questions, it is likely over. Remember, a good question asked at the wrong time is actually a bad question. At this time, a bad question would look like any of these:

Why am I doing this?

Is starting this what God has for me?

Do I have a plan to make this happen?

Is this worth the risk?

Why don't I have the support of my closest friends and family?

Am I willing to work overtime to see this venture succeed?

The reason these are now bad questions is that you are asking them at the wrong time. You already established the answers to these questions. You already know why you are starting this ministry. You already know God wants you to do this. You already know it's worth the risk. You know why your family thinks you're crazy. You already asked these good questions at the right time, but when things get tough these are no longer good questions. A good question at this point must help you figure out a way around your problem and to reach your previously agreed upon goal. Here are some good questions:

Why are we out of money?

How did we raise the most money in the beginning, and how can I do that again?

Did we not follow up with that donor like we said we would?

Is there something better than a fundraising dinner we could do?

Is there someone I can bring into a creative meeting to come up with new ideas?

As a mentor of mine says, at this point you are only one idea away from breakthrough. Asking good questions is about finding the one idea that could turn everything around. Asking bad questions brings self-doubt into the equation. Asking good questions

brings creativity. Bad questions bring fear. Good questions bring
hope. After establishing your direction with good questions, don't
destroy everything with bad questions. Ask good questions and get
out of your own way.

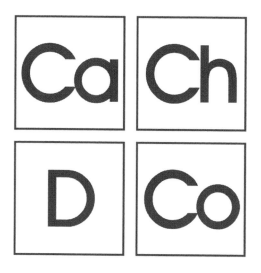

BRINGING THEM ALL TOGETHER

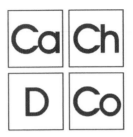

CHAPTER 10
THERE IS NO "I" IN "CHANGE THE WORLD"

"In union there is strength."
—DR. SEUSS

The Best There Ever Was

When I was growing up, I wanted to be a professional basketball player. There wasn't anything else that could be better than hitting the game-winning shot. The main reason for this was that I got to watch the greatest player in the history of the game play most of his career. He changed the face of the game forever, and his number—23—will forever be enshrined in Chicago.

I'm talking about Michael Jordan. I remember watching him win each of his six championships for the Chicago Bulls. I can remember when he closed his eyes during a game and made a free throw just to prove he was the best. I remember when he dropped 63 points in a single game. After winning three championships in a row, he suddenly retired and pursued his dream of playing baseball. After a year, he realized where he belonged and came back to the court. During the first year of his comeback, I got to see him play against the Atlanta Hawks.

My grandfather secured us a few tickets for the game, and I was as excited as I'd ever been. The seats were amazing—not quite at the half court line, only fifteen or so rows back. It was a dream come true. It was a very close game. Neither team took a lead of more than a few points. In the fourth quarter, with only a minute or so left, Chicago was up by one point. I turned to my grandfather and said it was over. Just like that, the Hawks stole the ball, went down, made a basket, and were up by one point with less than twenty seconds left in the game.

My grandfather turned to me and said, "Yep, it's over. Let's go."

He started to leave. I grabbed his arm and said, "No way! It's not over yet. Michael will win this game."

He sat back down, and I was a nervous wreck. I sat on the edge of my seat as the Bulls threw the ball in. Jordan dribbled the ball up the court, and the clock was ticking down. Ten seconds... nine seconds... eight seconds... there would only be time for one shot. With three seconds to go, Jordan made his move—he faked left, did a cross-over dribble back to his right, took the shot as the buzzer went off, and drained it! The Bulls won the game, and I got to see the greatest player in the world make the game-winning shot. I turned to my grandfather and said, "Now it's over!"

That shot is forever etched into my memory. There is no doubt that had it not been for Michael Jordan, the Bulls would not have won that basketball game, nor the six championships they won in a stretch of eight years. Jordan was the star. He was on SportsCenter and the cover of *Sports Illustrated*. He won the MVPs and was selected to the All-Star game. But for all the shots he made, if it hadn't been for the other players on the team, there would have been no championships, no MVP trophies, and no chance to hit the winning shot. Had it not been for John Paxson and Steve Kerr both hitting game-winning shots in the NBA Finals, you can take away two championships. Had it not been for Scottie Pippen, Horace Grant, and Dennis Rodman, there would have been no team, and with no team, there would have been no accomplishments. Just as you cannot win a basketball championship without a team, you cannot change the world without one either.

There's No "I" in "Change the World"

I want to end by highlighting the importance of the fact that you'll need a team to do something about it. There really is no such thing as the Lone Ranger when it comes to changing the world. No one did it on his or her own. It doesn't matter how skilled you are at multitasking, you get the same number of minutes in each day as everyone else—1,440. That's it. And once they're gone, they're gone forever. One of the greatest parts of including a team in your pursuit to change the world is that for every person who joins your team, you add 1,440 potential minutes that can be used to further the mission. If you have five people agree to join you in your efforts to (insert your passion or idea here), then you have 7,200 minutes that can be used to make it happen. Now, I know you're not going to spend every minute of the day working on your idea. You've got to sleep, eat, and take care of all the other parts of your life. My point is simply this: your time, which is your greatest asset, is also your most limited resource. The bigger your idea, the more help you'll need.

I always thought of the Apostle Paul as a trailblazing loner who only worked with a few people in his huge vision of taking the gospel to all the Gentiles. He had a few guys who helped, like Timothy, Titus, and Barnabas. I used to look at his ministry and think that I could lead the same way. I didn't need much help. I could do it all on my own. But this all changed when I read 2 Timothy recently. Paul wrote:

> Do your best to come to me quickly, for Demas, because he loved this world, has deserted me and has gone to Thessalonica. Crescens has gone to Galatia, and Titus to Dalmatia. Only Luke is with me. Get Mark and bring him with you, because he is helpful to me in my ministry. I sent Tychicus to Ephesus… Greet Priscilla and Aquila and the household of Onesiphorus. Erastus stayed in Corinth, and I left Trophimus sick in Miletus. Do your best to get here before winter. Eubulus greets you, and so do Pudens, Linus, Claudia and all the brothers. (2 Timothy 4:9–12, 19–21)

You can't read that and not see the huge number of people involved in Paul's ministry at the time he wrote the letter to Timothy. He was sending some people to other cities. He wanted Mark to come work directly with him. There were other people who he wanted to send greetings to for the past help they had given, and most likely were still continuing to give, to that day. Paul mentioned seventeen different people in his closing remarks to Timothy. How many of you would like to have seventeen people working on your idea with you? Imagine the amount of work you could get done if you had an extra 24,480 minutes to use.

When we look at the amount of work Paul accomplished in his ministry, we cannot overlook the help he had along the way. This is not meant to diminish what Paul accomplished; on the contrary, it speaks to his greatness as a leader. Only secure leaders who are confident in their calling will reach out for help. For they know that in growing the team, eventually they will increase their impact.

You will go further with a team than you will by yourself. This may not be evident in the beginning—it actually may be harder in the beginning. This most likely means you need to learn how to lead a team. You need to learn the art of delegating, motivating, and casting the right vision. If you delegate to people's areas of strength and cast a compelling vision, you will not be disappointed. A great place to start is to look where your greatest weaknesses lie. You have good ideas, you just need to put them in motion. If you are a visionary, you need a strategic thinker. If you are not organized, find someone who is. If you are poor at presentations, find someone who is good. Fill your weaknesses with the strengths of other people.

Three "C's" of Building a Team

In his modern classic, *Courageous Leadership*, Bill Hybels shares what he calls the three "C's" of building a dream team. When you are looking to grow the team, this is a good filter to run all applicants through. If they don't meet all three criteria, you should probably hold out until you find someone who does.

The first "C" is character. We've already talked about the importance of developing your own character. The same is true when building your team. You want to trust your team members. Every person who joins your team, whether you know it or not, is actually a walking billboard for your vision. People will connect that person to you and your vision whether you want them to or not. So it is important that you find someone with character. Remember, character is not who the person wants to be, but who the person actually is.

The next "C" is competence. The person you are recruiting needs to bring a certain skill to the team. They need to fill a need on the team. Don't just add another body. Add someone who is great at what they do. Don't be afraid to aim high. Once again, the larger your vision is, the better skills you will need. If you are planting a church and looking to build a staff, find a children's minster who not only loves kids but is also great at what he or she does. If you are looking for an executive director, find someone with a track record of amazing management skills. The point is not to skimp.

If they have character and competence, then the last "C" is chemistry. Hybels says that one of the reasons he enjoys ministry so much is that he loves working with the people on his teams. A person of chemistry gets along with you and the other team members. The last thing you want on your plate is to manage a troublemaker, pouter, or person with a negative attitude. These people are draining and will hold you and your team back from fulfilling your huge dream. There's not enough time to deal with that. Do your homework. Check references. Ask the other members of your team. Build a team that loves to be around each other. Add character and competency and you'll be well on your way to changing the world.

Accountability—You'll Want to Quit

In the twenty-year fight William Wilberforce endured to abolish slavery, there was a key moment in the journey that almost made him quit. After another frustrating defeat in the House of Commons, the spirit of Wilberforce and his whole team was crushed. They'd worked so hard only to come up short again. Wilberforce took some time off, and one of his loyal teammates, Clarkson, who had been fighting since the beginning, disappeared for a short while. A few months later, Wilberforce was at his home when Clarkson came riding up, joyful beyond belief. He had an idea, and Wilberforce needed to hear it. He had come up with an idea that would help their efforts to end the slave trade. It would not abolish it altogether, but it would be a big step in the right direction. The plan was to slip a small bill about ship flags into another trade bill. At the time, slave traders were flying under illegal flags. With the new bill, the Navy could stop and search these ships. This would make it harder for slave ships to get to port. It was an ingenious idea that worked.

When you are fighting for something as big as abolishing slavery and you are a decade into the fight, you will be tempted to quit. Probably numerous times. Wilberforce was trying to take down the backbone of the economy, which would be like trying to abolish the sale of gasoline today. Add to the fact that Britain at the time was fighting Napoleon in France, who was benefiting from slavery and you can see the uphill battle he was facing—I'm sure Napolean would have loved for England to end its slave trade, giving him an advantage in the war!

It was during this time that the team alongside Wilberforce would not allow him to quit. It was Clarkson who came up with one final idea, and it worked. Had Clarkson not been there to hold Wilberforce accountable to his goals and vision, there was a good chance he would have given up. When you have a team around you, they will give you the encouragement and accountability needed to keep pushing for your dream. No one said it would be easy, and you'll need to hear that often.

Holy Pep Talk

Today may have been the day you woke up and asked yourself, "Why the heck am I doing this?" If not, don't worry—that day is coming. Every church planter has that day. The questions. The doubts. The frustrations. The meeting last night that didn't go as planned. The major financial supporter decided not to give. Your only staff member opted to take another job. The rental agreement fell through.

When that day comes, you begin to question why you started a church in the first place. You could have stayed at that other job with a nice salary and benefits. If you hadn't moved, your kids would still be attending the same school. If you hadn't started this church, everything would be better... or so you tell yourself.

I'd like to offer an alternative for that day—the day when you encounter resistance, doubt, or frustration. As I was reading through 1 Corinthians recently, I couldn't get past verse one: *"Paul, called to be an apostle of Christ Jesus by the will of God..."*

I'm sure there are all sorts of scholarly explanations for why Paul wrote this, but as I began to look at the introductions of Paul's other letters, I was struck with a thought. Before I explain, listen to how he opens his other letters:

> Paul, a servant of Christ Jesus, called to be an apostle and set apart for the gospel of God... (Romans 1:1)

> Paul, an apostle of Christ Jesus by the will of God... (2 Corinthians 1:1)

> Paul, an apostle—sent not from men nor by man, but by Jesus Christ and God the Father, who raised him from the dead... (Galatians 1:1)

> Paul, an apostle of Christ Jesus by the will of God... (Ephesians 1:1)

> Paul, an apostle of Christ Jesus by the will of God... (Colossians 1:1)

> Paul, an apostle of Christ Jesus by the command of God our Savior and of Christ Jesus our hope... (1 Timothy 1:1)

> Paul, an apostle of Christ Jesus by the will of
> God, according to the promise of life that is in
> Christ Jesus... (2 Timothy 1:1)

After Paul became an apostle of Jesus, his life did not get easier or more luxurious. In fact, from an outsider's perspective you could probably say it got worse. But Paul knew that his calling was from God and that he served a much greater purpose than himself. Paul was given the mission of taking the gospel to the ends of the Earth. That's a pretty amazing calling. As Paul did this, he ran into opposition, riots, torture, prison, beatings, snakes, liars, dirty politicians, and a host of other unpleasantries. I am sure there were times when Paul was woke up and asked, "Why the heck am I doing this? Why should I keep going? Where am I going to find the strength to go on?"

I think Paul may have started all his letters the way he did as a reminder of how he had gotten caught up in this mission and who was ultimately responsible for it. Think of it like a look-in-the-mirror pep talk: *God has called me, by his power, and if it's his will, then he must have a plan. And if God has a plan, then he'll get me through this.* Paul knew he was called by God for a great task, and in times of struggle and doubt he needed to be reminded.

Maybe that's where you are. Maybe you're running into struggle, doubts, or resistance in your calling. If this is you, take a few minutes to stop what you're doing and remind yourself who called you. Remind yourself that if God called you, he has a plan. Paul shows us that the greater the plan, the harder it will be to accomplish—but the impact will be greater as well. So if this is you, take heart that the one who has called you is the creator and sustainer of the entire world. He didn't promise it would be easy—just that he would always be there with you.

I'm not going to lie—this is an extremely hard idea to deal with if you are at one of those low points. I remember a few years into the ministry when donations were low, sign-ups were low, and all kinds of self-doubt camped out in my head. It was a dark time, but looking back I see it was a necessary time. During those moments, I needed to remind myself of who it was that called me.

So maybe you should start your day with something like this:

(Your name here), called to be a church planter by God, the creator of the Universe...

(Your name here), called to lead a new non-profit to help stop slavery...

(Your name here), called by God to be a youth minister in this small town...

(Your name here), called by God to be a loving spouse and parent...

(Your name here), called by Jesus to work in Corporate America and leverage his or her influence for the local church...

One last thing: Paul closes his first letter to the Thessalonians by saying, *"The one who calls you is faithful and he will do it"* (1 Thessalonians 5:24). Remind yourself of who it was that called you. He is greater than your problems, doubts, and fears. When you want to quit, remember who's in your corner. When you want to go back to the old job, remember who's got your back. When you want to close the doors, remember the one who called you.

CONCLUSION

*"How wonderful it is that nobody
need wait a single moment before
starting to improve the world."*
—ANNE FRANK

W hat is it that you can't stop thinking about? What is that one thing you would start if you knew you couldn't fail? What is it that you wish you could rid from the earth? What is it that keeps you up at night?

If you could do something about it, imagine how different life would be. Imagine how much more energy you'd have. Imagine living a life filled with passion.

If you haven't found it yet, go find it.

If you know what it is, what are you waiting for?

Change *it.*

Build *it.*

Stop *it.*

Promote *it.*

Cure *it.*

Solve *it.*

Create *it.*

Encourage *it.*

Start *it.*

Write *it.*

Further *it.*

End *it.*

Do something about *it!*

Changing the world is hard. If it was easy, everyone would do it. But you're not everyone. You are going to change the world. Whatever it is, you must go for it. But remember, passion is not enough.

NEXT STEPS

Speaking

Greg Darley is available to present the key concepts of *Passion Is Not Enough* to your group or event. Through a passionate presentation, Greg will inspire and challenge your audience to become the type of person capable of changing the world. Speaking engagements can consist of one-day events or multiple days, including retreats.

If you are interested in having Greg speak at your next event, please email info@backstageleadership.org.

Passion Is Not Enough for Groups

Trying to change the world is best done with the help of others. We offer tools to facilitate group discussions for small groups, youth groups, and teams. We also offer discounts for bulk orders. For bulk orders, email info@backstageleadership.org.

Passion Is Not Enough Series

Host a 4-part *Passion Is Not Enough* series called "Becoming a World Changer." This series covers the four foundational elements required to change the world. For information on theme and content, email info@backstageleadership.org.

NOTES

[1] Belmonte, Kevin. *William Wilberforce: A Hero for Humanity* (Grand Rapids, MI: Zondervan, 2007), p. 151.
[2] Wikipedia contributors. "Butterfly effect." *Wikipedia, The Free Encyclopedia*. Wikipedia, The Free Encyclopedia, 4 Oct. 2010. Web. 5 Oct. 2010.
[3] Ibid.
[4] 1 Timothy 4:16.
[5] Goodwin, Doris Kearns. *Team of Rivals: The Political Genius of Abraham Lincoln* (New York, NY: Simon and Schuster, 2005), p. 52.
[6] Ibid.
[7] This is funny of God, because Egypt had not been mentioned in the conversation as of yet. Moses was just working with the sheep when God appeared. But Moses hadn't mentioned it. Maybe he was still thinking about it. Maybe his passion was still alive and God capitalized on it.

Appendix

For more information about individuals and organizations mentioned in the book:

Essential2Life works directly with families in the public housing communities of Atlanta—a city that comprises a disproportionate 43% of the region's poor. Since its inception, E2L has created mentoring and educational opportunities for over 10,000 youth. It is E2L's goal to help at-risk youth **"be more."**

www.E2Lonline.com

# HELP-PORTRAIT

The goal of Help-Portrait is simple: 1. Find someone in need, 2. Take their portrait, 3. Print their portrait, and 4. Deliver their portrait. Help-Portrait was formed by celebrity photographer Jeremy Cowart as he contemplated using his skills and expertise to give back to those who may not have the opportunity for a professional photo. The idea is that a photographer has the opportunity to help someone smile, laugh, and to remember—it is a movement, a shift in photography.

www.Help-Portrait.com

LAUNDRY LOVE PROJECT™

Laundry Love Projects (LLPs) are regular opportunities to help people who are struggling finan-
cially by assisting them with doing their laundry.
Relationships are built, and LLPs become small
communities of concern in which participants often
find that they receive assistance and benefit with
other areas of their lives.

http://just4one.org/laundrylove/

end child sex slavery & exploitation

Love146 works toward the abolition of child sex slavery and exploitation through Prevention and Aftercare solutions while contributing to a growing abolition movement.

www.Love146.org

PRISON
FELLOWSHIP

Prison Fellowship is a national nonprofit organization founded in 1976 by former Nixon aide Charles Colson. Colson was incarcerated for Watergate-related charges and could not forget those he had left behind those prison walls. He launched Prison Fellowship to give prisoners the opportunity to experience the radically transforming power of Christ that he had already experienced.

www.PrisonFellowship.org

BACKSTAGE
LEADERSHIP

Behind the scenes with today's top influencers, you get to ask amazing leaders any question you want. But the learning process does not end there. Unlike other learning opportunities that stop at information, we help you get to application. Each month, our coaches help all participants find ways to apply what they are learning and then hold them accountable.

www.BackstageLeadership.org

Hoops of Hope is the world's largest free-throw marathon. Similar to a walk-a-thon, participants raise awareness and funds by shooting free throws for children who have been orphaned by HIV/AIDS. 100% of all funds raised go directly to care for orphaned children in highly affected areas. This year, participants from all over the world will shoot thousands of free throws to represent the thousands of kids orphaned each day.

www.HoopsofHope.org

PASSION
IS NOT ENOUGH
STUDY GUIDE

Coming

Spring 2011

Great for small group or individual study.

www.GregDarley.com/book

Made in the USA
Charleston, SC
21 February 2011